Growing your Pastor

Ron Gordon

CREATION
HOUSE
A STRANG COMPANY

GROWING YOUR PASTOR by Ron Gordon
Published by Creation House
A Strang Company
600 Rinehart Road
Lake Mary, Florida 32746
www.creationhouse.com

All Scripture quotations are from the King James Version of the Bible.

Cover design by Terry Clifton

Library of Congress Control Number: 2005928281
International Standard Book Number: 1-59185-824-0

First Edition

05 06 07 08 09 — 87654321
Printed in the United States of America

This book is dedicated to my praying wife who sacrificed much to allow time for our ministry and for writing this book. I also give great thanks to our now deceased grandparents who prayed us out of eternal damnation for sure!

CONTENTS

Behold, this is the joy of his way, and out of the earth shall others grow.

—JOB 8:19

PREFACE

At first, many may think being a part of *Growing Your Pastor* is near blasphemy. That we, as mere laymen attending church and serving under a pastor—a God-chosen, God-appointed, and God-anointed vessel of God—should not be a part. They are spiritual leaders in authority over our lives. How can we grow a pastor, and more so, could it even be right that we think we should be a part of the growing, learning, and leading process of a pastor? We aren't supposed to do that! It has to be wrong somehow.

> The disciple is not above his master, nor the servant above his lord.
>
> —MATTHEW 10:24

If you think you are better, more equipped, or more spiritual than your pastor, you need to do one of two things—repent and learn who and what you really are, or get a new pastor.

Most pastors are mighty men and women of God who walk in a great anointing of God. I am not better than they, and I will probably never pastor a church. I have not been called by God to be a pastor, but I can help grow one.

I am not a tomato, either, but I can grow one. Growing a pastor is just as simple as growing a tomato. Find what makes them grow and provide it. Just as God has set life and growth in the tomato seed, He has also done so in our pastors. God has preordained our pastor's growth. Your part is to provide the needed nourishment, the needed environment, and the time and season for his or her growth. Think of this, we know God makes every plant, animal, and man grow. He has set in place the spiritual and natural laws for them to do so. The most important part for us is that we don't stunt or stop the growth by our own shortcomings and failures. Take a good tomato seed and pray over it continuously. We could, in fact, get all of our religious friends to pray with us and then plant it in northern Alaska and see what happens. There are places, seasons, and soils all under God's law that will not be altered.

We need to seek the will of God for our pastors, our churches, and ourselves. Then, by the power of Jesus' name and through our denying the wants and weaknesses of our flesh, we can bring into place the will of God. Every spiritual growth process, every correction process, every seeking of God's will must start with us, not others. Look in the mirror first. It is more than likely always the best place to find shortcomings.

Chapter One

THE PASTORAL FARMER

Growing pastors is exciting, rewarding, and an extremely needful ministry. It is also a lost art, and sadly not taught in the normal church. Though there are many important aspects of growing a pastor, two of them stand heads above all others. We must have a good understanding of these before we can hope to learn the others.

First, growing a spiritual pastor is very similar to growing any natural plant or animal. This may sound like a ridiculous statement, but we will see the truth in this by understanding the following verses:

> Another parable put he forth unto them, saying, The kingdom of heaven is like to a grain of mustard seed, which a man took, and sowed in his field: Which indeed is the least of all seeds: but when it is grown, it is the greatest among herbs, and becometh a tree, so that the birds of the air come and lodge in the branches thereof.
> —MATTHEW 13:31–32

The understanding of this parable is of immense value to our own personal growth in Christ., as well as the growth of any pastor or church leader. Seeds, when grown, became the greatest among herbs. Here a man planted the seed in his field, and he would do nothing else except tend to the plant. That was the total involvement of man's part,

1

the greatness preordained in the seed was God's part. We can't change the seed, which is preordained by God. We must understand that we are to grow God's pastor and not ours. Let the greatest in them grow, without trying to undo what God has already done. God's will and plans for these pastors must be honored above all things. We must not attempt to grow what we want for a pastor. We, as well as pastors, will be able to become what God has called us to be when we let His greatness in us grow unhindered.

Secondly, we should keep in mind that the pastors we grow are for an eternal work. They are to be about God's business, proceeding in God's will and ways, not ours. We should keep this verse close to our hearts, as it's not to be taken lightly. If we are not careful, we can actually end up working against God.

> The fear of the LORD is the beginning of wisdom: and the knowledge of the holy is understanding.
> —PROVERBS 9:10

We must have a wholesome fear of God to grow one of His pastors. Every man, woman, and child that has been called by God must be respected, as well as assisted. It is an awesome responsibility to grow one of God's chosen. It can also be one of the most rewarding and blessed experiences of our Christian walk. God has always, and will continue to, bless those who help fulfill the call of His selected servants. This is serious business but can be one of the most honorable ministries that a servant of God can perform. When this call is undertaken, we are actually working with God and fulfilling His mandate. Oh how wonderful to be in His employment!

It is highly likely you are serious about your relationship with God, or you would not have purchased this book. I pray that it will be of benefit to you, your church, and your pastor. In reading, it will become extremely clear that I am very serious about the spiritual conditions of our church. Please understand that I am an evangelist. God has burdened my heart to exhort and edify the body of Christ. Hopefully, it will be in an encouraging manner. It will become evident that I care about everyone's souls; your feelings are someone else's works, not mine. If you need an apology when you get your feelings hurt, let me apologize now, several times in fact. I hope I get some people so angry they actually get up and do something.

We all must be able to look at many things in a different way, and we must really open ourselves up to what God has said in His Word to be able to change the world. Sometimes, this may conflict with what we thought we knew. That's ok! In fact, there are areas in which I may be wrong. However, I believe that as you read this book, it will prompt you to think, consider, and realize the needs of some areas that you may not have considered before. If we all can just do that according to God's Word, the effort will be worth it.

In all endeavors, worldly or spiritual, we must know what we are doing. Many professions take years of education, followed by many more years of training before being able to perform their tasks. Skill, derived from training, experience, and internship under a tutor, has no equal. Though you must have a good understanding of the whole Word of God, you will not need any formal training to help your pastor grow. In fact, I believe that for some, and probably many, a higher education will hinder them. It makes no difference how much education we may have. It makes no difference how many initials and doctorates are in our titles. Our titles and accomplishments make no difference. The truth is without the knowledge of the Word of God we are spiritual morons.

I am not against higher education, in fact I am all for learning and the more the better. There are many seminary schools, some are even available on-line, that teach the true Word of God that will benefit most all of us. There is no substitute for learning, either by experience or through education. A balance of both will make one usable in any endeavor. The key is not how much we learn, but what you learn, and then correctly applying what we know.

The best knowledge we can have about God comes from God. His Word is always real, and his teachings are always truth. Just like Jesus, the Word is alive. God is still in the teaching business. He changes not, and is not a respecter of persons. We must believe in God's Word and that He will give each of us what is needed for our personal growth and ministry.

O the depth of the riches both of the wisdom and knowledge of God! how unsearchable are his judgments, and his ways past finding out!

—Romans 11:33

For to one is given by the Spirit the word of wisdom; to another the word of knowledge by the same Spirit.

—1Corinthians 12:8

Given by the Spirit, this is the knowledge and the spirit of truth that will bring down barriers. It will destroy religious doctrines of man, allowing us to raise up mighty sons and daughters of God that can help grow not religious pastors, but godly pastors. These pastors will have a foundation of God and not a foundation of man.

This book may give you some knowledge and bring to light some of God's Word. It may, however, just point you in the right direction. It's my prayer that it will cause us all to think in a different way, and to search our hearts and minds. We must cast off years of tradition; all of man's added to and taken away heresy, along with every bit of Satan's influence on the church. It is wrong and must be exposed for what it really is: lies! There are many resources for us to use, such as people, books, computers, numerous magazines and articles, all of which have a place. For the most part however, if not the only part, the only resource you'll need is the Bible. We all must understand just what the Bible is. The power of the Creator is enormous; however, all Jesus used to defeat Satan is the Word.

All scripture is given by inspiration of God, and is profitable for doctrine, for reproof, for correction, for instruction in righteousness: That the man of God may be perfect, thoroughly furnished unto all good works.

—2 Timothy3:16–17

Jesus did not use any religious doctrine of His time and neither are we to do so; it will not work. Victory will not come in our lives and neither will any pastor be successful using man-made creeds, statements, doctrine, or denominational concepts and beliefs. When the enemy comes into our lives or our families, he comes to steal, kill, and destroy. We and our pastors had better know God's Word and not merely a church's statement of faith. We must never allow any other Word, church doctrine, or even advice from a well-meaning source to have priority over the written Word of God. This is a huge problem in our churches today. Many priorities of man's flesh have been placed above the priorities of God.

May I suggest we all start right here with a new habit? Do not take any scripture given to us without reading the verses before and the verses after the scripture quoted. This is so that you know what it is really saying. Many—and I do mean many—take a scripture out of context and try to make it say what they want it to say. Always make it a habit to know all you can about the scripture. Remember what we learned in school: who, when, where, what, and why. Apply these. The author, the time period, and who it was written to can all be helpful as well.

Again, the best help is prayer by asking God to reveal to us His meaning. It is His Word and it was written for us. It is just as important and real today as it was thousands of years ago. It's shameful that so many in the church have never really spoken to God. Many don't even believe He will speak to them. He will, and God still makes house calls! We must know and study the whole Bible. It's a complete instruction guide for our lives. To be effective, we must use it as a complete reference. A small part by itself may not always represent what is the whole truth. For example, you cannot take all the blessings and prosperity scriptures without keeping His commandments. Faith without works is dead, and the lukewarm will be spewed out of His mouth.

We know and believe that all Scripture is given by the inspiration of God. To be effective in our Christian walk, let alone growing our pastor, we must believe that. If you are now thinking, "Well I know that, but men chose what books were included, and man made the translations, and men make mistakes," then stop right here with any thought of growing your pastor and start growing yourself. Immature thoughts do not have a place in a grown, mature man or woman of God.

> For when for the time ye ought to be teachers, ye have need that one teach you again which be the first principles of the oracles of

God; and are become such as have need of milk, and not of strong meat. For every one that useth milk is unskilful in the word of righteousness: for he is a babe. But strong meat belongeth to them that are of full age, even those who by reason of use have their senses exercised to discern both good and evil.

—HEBREWS 5:12–14

This is serious, brothers and sisters; it's about the priests of the almighty God. This is not Sunday School 101. Please understand that if you are not grown to a place to accept and do this work, don't do it. Also understand it's okay if you're not. Read this book, place the Word of God that's in it into your heart, and grow in Christ. It is also good to know that after thousands of years, when the Dead Sea scrolls were found, they were exactly, to every letter and Word the same as that which is in our Bibles today. God has protected His Word, for us!

God created the heavens and earth, and all that are in it in six days, and on the seventh day He rested. Since then everything, including His Son, has been grown. We all must grow, from milk to meat, and this is according to the Word of God. We cannot let our enthusiasm get ahead of our personal growth. All of us want to help and serve God right now. You will be glad to hear that I believe that if we are careful, we can take some steps to help our pastor as we are growing ourselves. In fact, I'm pretty sure most of us have a lot of growing left to do. We must make our personal growth our first priority. Let me say again, *we must put our personal growth as our first priority.* We cannot do much until we grow ourselves. It is our growth and maturity in Christ that is required to grow a pastor.

Growth for us, as well as our pastors, will come from time spent in the Word of God and prayer. We just read where the Bible is the inspired Word of God and all knowledge, wisdom, and discernment come from God's Word. I cannot overemphasize the value and need for prayer and time spent in God's Word. Our prayers prayed in faith, believing, are the only means of God moving on our behalf. God is not moved by need, but by prayer and faith. Jesus defeated Satan by the Word of God. God's Word is not only an instruction manual for us, but is recorded as an example to follow. We must be examples also of God's Word in us. It will set us free, and if obeyed, will allow God to bless us. I believe that the following verse is one of the important keys to our spiritual growth, our pastors' growth, and the health of the church, Jesus' church.

> But there is a spirit in man: and the inspiration of the Almighty giveth them understanding.
>
> —JOB 32:8

We as a church do not have this and will keep failing until we do. God has been removed from our schools and our government buildings. We have become *not* a nation under God, but a nation without a place for God. Look what has happened in a few short years: abortions are occurring at an alarming rate. Today, the blood of five thousand babies will spill on our soil. This headline would have been unthinkable only a few short years ago. What has changed?

The people have changed. God did not change, nor did His commandments. Abortion became a debate about legalistic rights and not the will of God. Every decision based on the majority, man's intellect, what feels good, or a man or woman's rights is of Satan Yes, it's of Satan. Satan is adept, very adept, at what he does. He is about to bring the only nation that was under God to its destruction. Why? We have made man's rights and desires above the will of God. We have become a generation seeking after ourselves and not seeking after God. We now have same-sex marriages. We are being told, "They should have their rights," and who are we to criticize them? Our government and our sick and perverse entertainment industry have malignantly educated the masses to condone the sin of homosexuals—it is wrong. There are now even churches that have homosexuals as priests. Unfortunately, what is worse is that literally thousands upon thousands, who know this is wrong, still support the church because of a misguided sense of loyalty to the denomination. You may get mad; you may justify yourself; you can do anything you want. But if that is you, your choice has not been of God. It is a religious doctrine that will burn in hell. If that is you, you are serving Satan and working against God.

There are only two choices: the world and Satan or God and eternal life in heaven. There is not a neutral or middle ground. Jesus said, "He that is not with me is against me; and he that gathereth not with me scattereth abroad" (Matt. 12:30). As Scripture reminds us, indeed, we are either for or against Him. One little compromise and we have changed sides and started working for Satan and didn't even realize it. Where are the Shadrach, Meshach, and Abed-negos who will not bow? Who will stand for God in these days?

No matter what our denomination is, we will not find it in heaven. Please hear this: we are either a son or daughter of God, or we are Satan's child. It is as simple as that. We must know who we are in Christ. It will never be denominational, nor will it ever be anything that divides the body of Christ.

Let us again read the same verse with hearts and minds open to Christ.

> For when for the time ye ought to be teachers, ye have need that one teach you again which be the first principles of the oracles of God; and are become such as have need of milk, and not of strong meat. For every one that useth milk is unskilful in the word of righteousness: for he is a babe. But strong meat belongeth to them that are of full age, even those who by reason of use have their senses exercised to discern both good and evil.
>
> —HEBREWS 5:12–14

What has happened? To phrase it in a more factual context: what has not happened? What has not happened is that we are not a people, a church, or country that truly believes in God; and we are not willing to stand for what we know to be the truth. We have compromised the truth and willingly became a part of the majority. We needed to fit in; we had other agendas, not agendas for God, but many other agendas. Almost all, if not all, of these agendas were about us, our desires, and fulfilling man's lust. In doing so, we were and are serving Satan. To understand whose agenda was being promoted, all we have to do is see the fruit it produced. How much fruit have we allowed to be produced that is of Satan and not of God?

> That we henceforth be no more children, tossed to and fro, and carried about with every wind of doctrine, by the sleight of men, and cunning craftiness, whereby they lie in wait to deceive; But speaking the truth in love, may grow up into him in all things, which is the head, even Christ.
>
> —Ephesians 4:14–15

We, as a church and as a society, have allowed someone who is literally going to hell into our chuch. We as one church, one body, one head in Jesus Christ, have allowed ourselves and our country to be tossed to and fro by peoples' wills and peoples' rights that were put above God's commandments. We as a church, as a society, have allowed someone who is literally going to "burn in hell unless they repent" and "sin no more" the right to be above God's laws. We are commanded to love them, and we should; but we must never accept the sin as anything but sin. We must understand there are only two sides and always only two sides. When we don't speak out, don't protest, or do not take a stand for Jesus, it is the same as being against Jesus. If we are not for Him, we are against Him. Neither a minority nor a majority can change God's Word. The final judge will not be the nine people that are called the Supreme Court. In fact, I believe most of them are going to have a difficult time when they meet the real Judge. We need to include them in our prayers as we pray for our country. The highest court in the United States is serving Satan: the anti-Christ. Soon we are going to answer for this as a nation and as individuals who allowed this to happen.

> And likewise also the men, leaving the natural use of the woman, burned in their lust one toward another; men with men working that which is unseemly, and receiving in themselves that recompence of their error which was meet. And even as they did not like to retain God in their knowledge, God gave them over to a reprobate mind, to do those things which are not convenient; Being filled with all unrighteousness, fornication, wickedness, covetousness, maliciousness; full of envy, murder, debate, deceit, malignity; whisperers, Backbiters, haters of God, despiteful, proud, boasters, inventors of evil things, disobedient to parents, Without understanding, covenantbreakers, without natural

affection, implacable, unmerciful: Who knowing the judgment of God, that they which commit such things are worthy of death, not only do the same, but have pleasure in them that do them.

—ROMANS 1:27–32

This is the Word of God, and no vote, no state, and no country will change His Word. His Word is true: "For verily I say unto you, Til heaven and earth pass, one jot or one tittle shall in no wise pass from the law, til all be fulfilled" (Matt. 5:18). Heaven and earth will pass away, but the Word of God will stand forever, and forever will be unchanged. This is where we as a nation abandoned our forefathers' intentions, which were clearly to be a godly nation. We can never accept that sin is anything but sin. No matter how common it gets, sin is still sin. A majority vote does not change it. We must understand that we should love all sinners into the church—into the presence of God, instead of condemning them!

Recently a well-known and very respected man of God said, "Sixty percent of the people in our churches are not truly saved, and are going to burn in hell." It would really be sad if that was the country as a whole, but it is our churches! Oh, how we have failed! Are we too stupid, too religious, and too busy to even know that we are failing and why? We, the baby boomers in this country, have lost more ground to Satan and did so faster than any other generation since Adam and Eve. We are much worse than the Pharisees and Sadducees. We knew the truth and simply did nothing. We are nailing Jesus to the cross every day in this country. Every time we reject Him, again and again, we are re-crucifying Jesus.

We must be raising pastors that will speak the truth and speak out to those whose hope is tied to having tried to live a good life. A good life according to the morality of a lost and perverse nation, in reality, is a ticket to hell. People must know that they are going to burn in hell, along with all those without salvation. Heaven is only for the saved, those that are washed in the blood and changed by a true born-again experience with Jesus. Scripture promises salvation through Jesus: "That if thou shall confess with thy mouth the Lord Jesus, and shalt believe in thine heart that God hath raised him from the dead, thou shalt be saved" (Rom. 10:9).

Many are headed to hell because of a watered-down, feel-good message, from pastors and churches preaching their "feel-good" gospel. We need pastors that have the Word of God in them, and who love the people enough to tell them the truth; pastors who hear from God and speak only what God is saying, not what man wants to hear. We do not need pastors that are worried only about growth and offerings. This is a good place to help every pastor grow. Every time we see any person putting any needs or requirements above the spiritual needs and truth of God's Word, we need to assist them. They need to be taken aside in love and prayerfully corrected and then taught correctly. Intercede for your pastor and be in continuous prayer. Many people in the church simply do not know better, however, they want to better serve and be more useful. Help them. This helps the church and helps the pastor.

There is a fight; there is a war. And we must understand and prepare. Satan is trying to destroy your pastor, your church, and anything that would promote the kingdom of God. There are many churches and pastors who do not believe this and have never experienced an attack. The reason is that they are not doing anything that bothers Satan. In fact, many are doing more work for him than they are for God. If this is your church, change it or leave; do not become compliant or care more about the church than God's work. If you're going to serve God and grow godly pastors, you're going to make Satan mad. I hope I never stop making him mad. God, through Jesus Christ, gave us power over Satan for a reason, and that reason is to save souls. Use your power; it is the will of God for you to do so.

> For we wrestle not against flesh and blood, but against principalities, against powers, against the rulers of the darkness of this world, against spiritual wickedness in high places.
> —EPHESIANS 6:12

Our fight is against Satan and is never against a person or personality. We are to be servants—servants to God, servants to our pastors, and most of all, servants to the body of Christ. God pointed this out very early in His gospel; in fact, it may have been the very first question. He also answered the question that we are our brother's keeper and we need to act like it. We must serve, appreciating what our pastors are up against. Look at the pitiful condition of our nation as well as the entire world. The true church should set the standards of a nation. The church not only has failed, but has allowed the morality of a majority to set the standards of the church.

God forgive us! The majority of our next generation may well be lost. At this critical time when we are in need of godly pastors, they are leaving the pulpit at a rate of thousands every month. Many have just been beaten down, worn down, and pushed down by those they were called to help. They were called as servants also and were charged with the responsibility of our very souls. We were always there to receive, but some of us never have given back to them.

How did many in the church get the mind-set that life and life more abundantly is for the congregation and not the pastor? There was never an unmet need of any priest in the Bible. If we know God's Word, we know God doesn't change, so why did the church? We have the idea that every hardworking person should prosper except a man or woman of God. They are to be kept poor and in need of the church. Churches must understand that every law of God and every blessing is to be kept and shared by everyone. We are too stupid to understand that we need the pastors more than they need us.

> For it is written in the law of Moses, thou shalt not muzzle the mouth of the ox that treadeth out the corn. Doth God take care for oxen? Or saith he it altogether for our sakes? For our sakes, no doubt, this is written: that he that ploweth should plow in hope; and that he that thresheth in hope should be partaker of his hope. If we have sown unto you spiritual things, is it a great thing if we shall reap your carnal things? If others be partakers of this power over you, are not we rather? Nevertheless we have not used this power; but suffer all things, lest we should hinder the gospel of Christ. Do ye not know that they which minister about holy things live of the things of the temple? and they which wait at the altar are partakers with the altar? Even so hath the Lord ordained that they which preach the gospel should live of the gospel.
>
> —1 CORINTHIANS 9:9–14

We are to take the money earned from our carnal job and give to our church and pastors. According to Scripture, all jobs and occupations except priests/pastors are carnal. We can and should be doing good, godly things while at work, even though the job is carnal. We take the money we earn and purchase housing, food, clothing, and other necessities. The problem is never the job or money. The problem is when we take our first fruits, our tithes and offerings, and do not sow them into the house and pastor of God. Today, the worth of an entertainer or sports star, who offers a few moments of stimulation, is by and far worth more than the one who leads us to an eternal life in heaven in lieu of hell. We think that celebrities deserve their rewards while pastors who are blessed financially are looked upon as thieves. Many believe that pastors, as a whole, should not be prosperous.

We must understand that pastors do not need the churches. The churches need them. There are some church boards that take the average pay of the church members and pay the pastor accordingly. Now that's absurd! How can any average secular job ever equal to a God-appointed position? Worldly will never equal spiritual. Boards, you will answer to God. In fact, I believe that when the rewards are handed out in heaven, your attitude towards God's chosen will be pointed out. Do not expect more than you gave!

Here is a fact, please remember it. We can always look at the financial condition of a church's pastor and tell the spiritual condition of the church. Always! I'm not going to elaborate here because it's a different subject, but every one of us needs to learn that there are laws, God's laws, and they are unchangeable. The law of sowing and reaping is one. This is not only a law of quantity, but what seed you sow. Some of us have planted crops that we really do not want the harvest of. We will reap what we have sown. Selfishness, being opinionated, or being stubborn are harvestable crops just like gossip or pornography. Sowing and reaping is not limited to finances. One of the biggest crops reaped in the church today is the "done nothing" crop, and they reap manyfold "nothing!"

There are many congregations and church boards that need to understand that to grow your pastor you first have to keep them! It's hard for a pastor to pray for the needs of the members when he has to pray for a new pair of shoes for his kids. Pastors also need enough money to pay the gas bill they ran up visiting people in the hospital. Many times, they are visiting relatives or friends of ours that do not even attend their church. It is the responsibility of each and every one of us to provide the pastor's needs.

> I am crucified with Christ: nevertheless I live; yet not I, but Christ liveth in me: and the life which I now live in the flesh I live by the faith of the Son of God, who loved me, and gave himself for me.
> —GALATIANS 2:20

The church, the body of Christ, must understand this if we are to accomplish what God has set before us to do. It says, "By the faith of the Son of God," and yes we are to have faith, but even God did not feed Elijah by faith.

> And it shall be that thou shalt drink of the brook; and I have commanded the ravens to feed thee there. So he went and did according unto the word of the LORD: for he went and dwelt by the brook Cherith, that is before Jordan. And the ravens brought him bread and flesh in the morning, and bread and flesh in the evening; and he drank of the brook.
> —1 KINGS 17:4-6

Many ministries have been ruined when money began to pour in because of a lack of management and spiritual growth in that ministry. What happens? Here is an area where we, as the church, think that the pastor can be all things. Pastors can't, and you and I need to accept it.

Jesus did not keep the purse; neither did He go after the money to pay the taxes. He had others to do and to go. Today, "the others" are you and I. However, the pastors need to be well-blessed themselves. It's the church's responsibility to do this. It's our responsibility, because God gave it to us to do, and we are God's modern-day ravens.

If you are serious (which I'm sure you are if you're reading this book) about church growth and about kingdom growth, it is up to us to help others to understand these spiritual concepts. It may be helpful to understand we cannot find a successful church anywhere in the developed countries where the pastor is poor. It's simply against the laws that God has set in place. God will bless the people that bless His chosen. He does it for Israel, and He'll do it for His church, anywhere. To grow our pastor, we must start by blessing him with finances, as well as prayer.

In order for our churches to grow, set godly examples, and become the leaders of humanity, we need to first stop the mass exodus of our pastors from the pulpit. There are two key points that I feel would really help with this situation. First, every person who has any say over a pastor should never make a decision without fasting for three to seven days and seeking the will of God. If you are not willing to do this on a regular basis, you are not capable of making decisions that are of God. Never serve God with less than all you have and all you can be. Seek other areas of service if you have not yet grown to handle these needed requirements to be responsibly capable.

Secondly, and more importantly, pastors need to remember this verse:

> And Jesus said unto him, No man, having put his hand to the plough, and looking back, is fit for the kingdom of God.
> —Luke 9:62

Am I trying to say that a person who is truly—and I mean truly—called to preach and that gives up and quits is unfit for the kingdom of heaven? No, I am not, but God did. Pastors, do you really think God changed His mind because of your personal situation? Did you go through something that others haven't endured, or did Satan just win you over? You wanted to preach the gospel, however, sometimes we have to live it to preach it.

I am here writing a book about pastors, after having my heart torn apart by one. Why? Because God said to. It is not about me or that pastor. Many of the great men in the Bible suffered real sufferings. In situations of real suffering, you're in good company; learn, grow up, and go on. If you have not been skinned alive or boiled in oil, quit crying and start preaching. Start by thanking God for the fact that your circumstances were not worse. Pray for forgiveness for failing a test you know you should have passed. Move on if the church you are at, or were at, will not accept correction. Shake the dust off and go where they will accept your teaching. The world has many times more people that are lost than saved; you will not live long enough to run out of areas. Go! Pastors you know the Word of God is true. You know God does not change and you know you're going to stand at the judgment bar of Christ. Let's hope the words spoken to you will be, "Good and faithful servant" instead of, "You're not fit for the kingdom of God." Here's a great piece of advice: get back to work! People are dying and going to hell because of your lack!

When we do not know the Word of God, we cannot tell a lie from the truth, and this lack of knowledge is dangerous. We say, "Well that surely can't be. God sent His Son because He loves us." Yes, He did. He has also killed more people than all the wars put together that men have fought, did so very quickly, and has done so often.

Pastors, either you were to change the conditions of the people and failed, or you simply missed God and were at the wrong place or possibly it was the wrong time. Every pastor is going to get it wrong once in awhile; move on, but move on with God and in God. For if God is for you, who can be against you? I believe, pastors, that every promise in the Bible is for you also, and even more so. You were handpicked by God and should be acting accordingly.

> The fear of LORD is the beginning of knowledge: but fools despise wisdom and instruction.
>
> —PROVERBS 1:7

> The fear of the LORD prolongeth days: but the years of the wicked shall be shortened.
>
> —PROVERBS 10:27

Earlier I mentioned that a higher education may hinder many. Education certainly has not been beneficial for the United States at this time. Look at us as a nation. We are the most educated generation with the most resources for learning. We have been afforded immense opportunities to expand the kingdom of God and to save untold thousands of thousands, even millions. We have, however, chosen to lean toward our own understanding and knowledge and to chase after our own lusts. We, as a nation, have been expending the will of man and Satan by trusting in the knowledge and understanding Satan presents. All we have to do is just look at every media there is. You'll see more of Satan's work than of God's work. You would think we would at some point get the idea that Satan is a liar, and everything of him is a lie.

Right now the king of the United States is Budweiser, however, the real King of kings will return. He will judge and judge righteously, and it will not be by the Supreme Court, or popular opinion, or the will of the people. We are either for God or against Him! We are either reaping or scattering. We must be helping our brothers and sisters to understand this. It must start with us, the church body. We are the ones who are to keep God's commandments. We are to discern the truth and proclaim it loudly and boldly. It is time to be screaming: "This is wrong and we will not stand for it anymore. We will stand for God, and only God!"

Before I could help myself grow and before I could be of any help to any pastor, I had to make some hard choices and come to some realizations about myself. I could only grow in God and God's will for my life as I died to myself. I had to forget all that I used to build a business. All that I thought I knew was of no use to God. If God could not use me, neither could I be of any help to a pastor. Instead of being a help, I was in need of being helped. I was as all new Christians are: I was like a baby that needed to be fed milk and be taken care of. Instead of being able to teach, I had to be taught.

I thank God for having provided a teaching pastor for me. We need to trust that God will provide us what we need and provide it all when we need it. Many times we do not grow and receive what God has for us because we are fighting to be where we want, getting what we want. We must let go and trust God!

If we are really serious, we must first understand that to work successfully and fully in the kingdom of God, all that we are, all that we know, and all of our capabilities and knowledge are of no or little use. This is completely different than everything we have learned to be successful in the world. If you want to be used by God, offer yourself as an empty vessel to be broken, fired, and remade by God. (See Romans 9:19–22.) We must empty ourselves of us and the worldly knowledge we have learned. The more of us there is, the less there is for God to use. If we think we are really good, really smart, with a lot of capabilities, God cannot use us, for our natural abilities without God's presence or our own spiritual insight from Him are useless to Him. Only in God's power—or in His abilities working through us—are we able to do His will.

> Arise, and go down to the potter's house, and there I will cause thee to hear my words. Then I went down to the potter's house, and, behold, he wrought a work on the wheels. And the vessel that he made of clay marred in the hand of the potter: so he made it again another vessel, as seemed good to the potter to make it. Then the word of the LORD came to me, saying, O house of Israel, cannot I do with you as this potter? saith the LORD. Behold, as the clay is in the potter's hand, so are ye in mine hand, O house of Israel.
>
> —JEREMIAH 18:2–6

We must learn to be unlearned. We must literally die to ourselves and become new creatures. Here is a key point we need to learn and remember. Without dying to ourselves, we cannot be living for God.

> Therefore if any man be in Christ, he is a new creature: old things are passed away; behold, all things are become new.
>
> —2 CORINTHIANS 5:17

God is looking for people who will submit to His will and His understanding. To do this, we must allow ourselves to be remade just as we were reborn into salvation. Forget how you can do it, and allow it to be done by His Spirit. We must come to the point of understanding that everything we have ever done well was of God, and the rest was of us. We are nothing and never will be anything in and of ourselves. The very best I can ever hope to be is a vessel acceptable for God to use with a mind not of my own, but the mind of Christ.

> But he that is spiritual judgeth all things, yet he himself is judged of no man. For who hath known the mind of the Lord, that he may instruct him? but we have the mind of Christ.
>
> —1 CORINTHIANS 2:15–16

What we can do when we learn that we can't do anything? We must know that He that is in us can do all things! We know nothing, but our God knows all things. We are not to understand, but to obey and stand, and then stand some more.

> Wherefore take unto you the whole armour of God, that ye may be able to withstand in the evil day, and having done all, to stand. Stand therefore, having your loins girt about with truth, and having on the breastplate of righteousness.
> —EPHESIANS 6:13–14

To grow our pastors we must know who gives us the knowledge, the power, and what part we are to play in the process.

> I can do all things through Christ which strengtheneth me.
> —PHILIPPIANS 4:13

It is only by Christ, and only in Christ, that we can do anything at all. When we get to this point, we can help our pastors grow as well as grow ourselves. These verses, some of which we just read, bear reviewing with a new understanding.

> That we henceforth be no more children, tossed to and fro, and carried about with every wind of doctrine, by the sleight of men, and cunning craftiness, whereby they lie in wait to deceive; But speaking the truth in love, may grow up into him in all things, which is the head, even Christ.
> —EPHESIANS 4:14–15

When our feelings get hurt, we must understand that it's not our feelings that are important, but how we handle things. It's about Jesus. Jesus wants us to pray for the one who hurt us and love them more. We will act like Jesus and always forgive, always love.

> As newborn babes, desire the sincere milk of the word, that ye may grow thereby: If so be ye have tasted that the Lord is gracious. To whom coming, as unto a living stone, disallowed indeed of men, but chosen of God, and precious, Ye also, as lively stones,

are built up a spiritual house, an holy priesthood, to offer up spiritual sacrifices, acceptable to God by Jesus Christ. Wherefore also it is contained in the scripture, Behold, I lay in Sion a chief corner stone, elect, precious: and he that believeth on him shall not be confounded. Unto you therefore which believe he is precious: but unto them which be disobedient, the stone which the builders disallowed, the same is made the head of the corner, And a stone of stumbling, and a rock of offence, even to them which stumble at the word, being disobedient: whereunto also they were appointed. But ye are a chosen generation, a royal priesthood, an holy nation, a peculiar people; that ye should shew forth the praises of him who hath called you out of darkness into his marvellous light.

—1 PETER 2:2–9

Thank God you were chosen for just such a time as this. Ask God to help you fulfill the purpose He has chosen for you. If you're serious about this, it should not be some happenstance prayer. Get real, do some fasting, seek God, and get on your face before God. I have heard from God more with my face buried in the carpet at my sanctuary, than with raised eyes and hands. We must learn to become humble and broken and determined to be open to newness and anointing to serve Him that called us.

But grow in grace, and in the knowledge of our Lord and Savior Jesus Christ. To him be glory both now and for ever. Amen.

—2 PETER 3:18

Is it possible for us to come together as a people, as a part of the body of Christ, as fellow servants of God, and as servants to our pastors with this understanding? Yes! We can and must! It will only happen when we are no longer *we*, but when it is He that is in us! Then and only then are we servants of God.

I can and will do all things through Christ. I am the head and not the tail. I can have life and have it more abundantly. My pastor will grow and grow in Christ. We must get to the point where we are Christlike, so our pastor can be more Christlike. We are to be imitators of Christ; in fact, we are to be imitators of God. Some will say, "Oh no, this is blasphemy." No, that is of the devil. I was made by God and in the likeness of God. I am His son, an heir to the kingdom with Jesus. It is mine. God wanted me to have it. Jesus paid a high price for it and I will not waste it. I also want our pastors to have everything God has for them. It is my duty to eliminate every hindrance possible that would keep a blessing of God from reaching my pastor. May I suggest this be your goal as well: that we all help to do everything possible to insure our pastors receive all of God's blessings. The truth is very simple, either we are these things and can do these things in Jesus' name, or we belong to the devil. To whom do we belong?

We must put our pastors in their place. We must understand their place, and keep them in their place.

> Remember them which have the rule over you, who have spoken unto you the word of God: whose faith follow, considering the end of their conversation. Jesus Christ the same yesterday, and to day, and for ever.
>
> —HEBREWS 13:7–8

The place for our pastors is in authority. They are charged with our very souls. They are the chosen of God. They are responsible to God and not to man. Our pastors must be in tune with God, hearing from God. Many can't hear God over the noise of their congregation's complaints. How can they hear the small, still voice of God over our yelling, complaining, and our neediness? Is it possible that we simply understand God knew we would need pastors and that we were going to need help? Accept this gift of God as it truly is. It is from God and not by the board or committee. We need to thank God daily for a godly pastor, and be continuously speaking good things into our pastors' lives.

> I exhort therefore, that, first of all, supplications, prayers, intercessions, and giving of thanks, be made for all men; For kings, and for all that are in authority; that we may lead a quiet and peaceable life in all godliness and honesty. For this is good and acceptable in the sight of God our Saviour; Who will have all men to be saved, and to come unto the knowledge of the truth.
>
> —1 TIMOTHY 2:1–4

How much time every day and every week do you spend in prayer for your pastor? There is nothing more important, and more so in this day and time, than ever before. It is unthinkable for me to have my pastor step up to a pulpit without prayer!

I was going to a church once where I and others were praying at every service. We prayed not only for the pastor, but also for everyone who preached or taught. The pastor had even been warned by more than one prophecy how very much Satan was after him and the church. Music practice and programs became more important than prayer. It was, in fact, pointed out that the people doing the praying were interfering. Prayer stopped, and Satan attacked the pastor and the church in less than two weeks. God had great plans for that pastor that may never be fulfilled. What God had set in place for him to do, now very well may be done by others in his place. This is real. Prayer is real and it works!

If we want to grow our pastor, do not let him do anything without our prayers—and not just happenstance prayers! I mean real prayer, on your knees, in a group, all in one accord! Pray during the service. Every good pastor will encourage and welcome prayer for all that they do. Find a pastor who feels that he does not need your prayers and run from him! That pastor cannot be a vessel of God.

> And when he putteth forth his own sheep, he goeth before them, and the sheep follow him: for they know his voice. And a stranger will they not follow, but will flee from him: for they know not the voice of strangers.
>
> —JOHN 10:4–5

Do not wait! Flee from the man or woman who does not want prayer! Know for sure that there are devils in our pulpits, that they are fulfilling Satan's agenda, not God's!

> Servants, be obedient to them that are your masters according to the flesh, with fear and trembling, in singleness of your heart, as unto Christ; Not with eyeservice, as menpleasers; but as the servants of Christ, doing the will of God from the heart; With good will doing service, as to the Lord, and not to men: Knowing that

whatsoever good thing any man doeth, the same shall he receive of the Lord, whether he be bond or free.

—EPHESIANS 6:5–8

We as a church can conquer the world for God, instead of losing our own country to Satan, by following these four little verses: Our pastors are not deities, nor are they to be raised up on some pedestal. They are, however, our masters. Just as Christ is the head; our pastors are the head. As we treat our pastors when we speak of them, we are treating and speaking to Jesus himself. We need to remember that before opening our mouths the next time. How can we read of God's chosen servants in the Bible with such awe and show so little respect for those whom He has chosen in these last days? We, you and I, were born for this time! This is a wonderful time to serve our Lord! I believe we are really in the last days. There are wars and spiritual wars to be fought. (See 2 Timothy 3:1–5.) We were born at a time and in a place to be a part of the End Times fight. Can we even begin to understand how important we and our pastors are for such a time as this? It's time for a revival, and this revival needs to be started by only two people. It's already started in me, and now in you. Let it be called the revival of the pastor farmers.

Chapter Two

KNOW YOUR CROP
BEFORE YOU GROW

What is it that we want to grow? What kind of pastor do we want, and is what we want what we really need? These seem like simple questions that are readily answerable. This is, however, where so many problems arise. We need only to open up our phone books and look under churches. The yellow pages of the Orlando, Florida phone book have 142 different headings for churches. The Baptists alone claim 15 different types of headings. We must ask ourselves how many different or similar denominations should there be? Are these all God's churches? What's worse is how many of the same denominations are located so close together. These churches are almost always struggling to survive and seem to never have any finances or time to give to missions. We all must understand the real mission of any church is souls, restoring lives, and raising up leaders to be released to go into the world.

The root of one of the prevalent problems in our churches lies in these two key questions: what do we want to grow and what kind of pastor do we want? What is missing is what God wants. We have failed miserably at relinquishing our wants for God's.

It would be a wonderful situation if all the church buildings were full. It's not only sad, but possibly even a sin that most of the denominations, and most of the individual church buildings exist with little or no unity. If there is a difference of opinion, a new one springs up down the street. This is not, nor has it ever been, the plan of God for His church.

Let's get realistic! Jesus is going to return for one church, without spot or wrinkle. Scripture tells us: "That he might present it to himself a glorious church, not having spot, or wrinkle, or any such thing; but that it should be holy and without blemish" (Eph 5:27). It is not going to be my church or your church, but His glorious church! How many souls could we reach with just the finances spent keeping up these self-surviving churches that are only blocks apart? I am sure that we can all sympathize with these churches and their members. They have friends. They are used to having church their way. Some have been going there so long it's a natural habit now.

The fact is, many have not done a thing to expand the kingdom of God and are doing more for Satan than God! How can we ever explain this at our hour of judgment, when so many are perishing right now into hell? Many of these churches are a social club acting like a church. They are fake and counterfeit and belong to Satan.

If we can mature enough to see the reality of this in the spiritual world, we would start to understand the true consequences of this abomination! There are thousands upon thousands of these churches consuming the finances needed to reach the lost world. These are good men and women. Many are wanting and willing to be used, but the financial conditions of their churches won't allow anything to be done. We see this repeated many thousands of times over, and we must understand Satan's role in this. At times it involves loyal and sincere brothers and sisters in Christ, with the greatest of intentions, but they all appear to lack one thing. They cannot produce any fruit for God. Can we even begin to imagine what would happen if we put aside our differences, forgot about a man-made church, and all joined together as one body and one church for Jesus? We would start taking back our towns, and country, as well as saving our children and families! We must start casting off pride and a false sense of loyalty to a building or group, and become the mighty and powerful church God has set for us to be. This is going to take mighty pastors that are capable of seeing the overall picture. Will we see the day when churches, just blocks apart, come together in love? Will we see churches that are spiritual enough to simply close their doors and join with other congregations to become more capable of performing God's calling on His church? This is when we will manifest Christ in us and in our churches. This is when the flesh of man will give way to the Spirit of God.

> And Jesus knew their thoughts, and said unto them, Every kingdom divided against itself is brought to desolation; and every city or house divided against itself shall not stand: And if Satan cast out Satan, he is divided against himself; how shall then his kingdom stand?
>
> —MATTHEW 12:25–26

Jesus is teaching us a very important lesson that we have yet to learn. We cannot survive as a divided church. We are to be one church, in unity. A church split, one that removes a pastor due to anger, pride, or ill feelings that cause division, is of Satan and not of God.

Remember this: it is important and always true that if it is not in love, it is not of God. Scripture tells us: "He that loveth not knoweth not God; for God is love" (1 John 4:8).

So many churches have been formed from the discord of splitting the body of the church. Few want to acknowledge that, after Jesus, the pastor is the head. When they split the body and leave, they become a headless freak. They have no head, and most have become an unwilling and unknowing servant of Satan, doing his works. Spiritual growth will allow us to see past the present state or problem, giving way to prayer and faith in God, working out the problems. Can we see that this happens because we did not spend enough time in prayer? Do we realize that it may be because we just did not believe God would answer our prayers and resolve whatever the issue was? Invariably, church splits are headed up by those that, we could say, are petite in spirit and abundant in mouth.

Why are there so many problems? First and foremost is the lack of spiritual maturity. Secondly, we don't understand how to handle

27

chastisement or rebuke from our pastors. There are, of course, pastors who are failing in their calling and refuse proper correction. Pride in a pastor is an awful thing. This needs to be corrected. But the correction should start with love and prayer and for the good of God's kingdom. It should then be corrected. Correction should be done to build up and perfect the person, not to tear down and destroy. We have all fallen short and will probably do so again. We should edify and encourage in a perfecting manner, under the leadership of the church whose agenda is Christ and not a personal one.

The Word of God cuts likes a two-edged sword, cutting deep. (See Hebrews 4:12.) Instead of receiving that which we need to be a better Christian, we let pride get in our way. When a pastor or church leader hurts our feelings by rebuking us, we take our lack, our own falling short, out on the messenger instead of growing from the message. Hurt feelings nearly always turn into anger. We must be able to love one another and work with one another if we are to serve our Lord. This should be from the top down, beginning with pastors treating us all in love.

The third reason there are so many problems within the church is because we have raised or transplanted the wrong species. Let us look at a pastor like a tree. How many types of trees are there? Some grow edible fruit, some are for shade, some grow fast, some slow, some in cold elements, some in moderate, and some only in hot climates. Besides these, some grow in poor soil, some in rich soil, some in dry conditions, and some in wet. The differences are endless. Keeping this in mind, let's make it simple. We'll just decide on an apple tree. Let's all agree we will grow a pastoral apple tree. Let's start with a seed, or should we start with a seedling? We could start with a tree that is already producing fruit.

Let us review the choices starting with a seed. If your pastor is a seed, or a young seedling in need of potting, he will require much care. This type of pastor has no roots or leaves yet and is incapable of feeding himself. Every pastor has to start here. It's sad how many die in this stage before they get rooted and grow leaves and become self-sustaining. For cultivated plants, almost all early deaths are due to how the cultivator handled the plant. In the case of pastors, the cultivators are their parents, family, and friends. Many of the pastors who survive this early stage are later killed by really religious church people who know all there is to know. We all know some of these people. They are in most churches. They are the same type that are in most neighborhoods and workplaces. Wherever they are, everything is always about them. They always know how to tell someone what to do and are seldom seen doing anything themselves. Authority and attention are what motivate them.

We are to love these kinds of people and pray for them, but when we let them control anything spiritual, let alone a pastor, it is bound to fail. They are doing the work of Satan. It's time they are sat down and fed the Word of God in love. Remove them from any place of authority now. Why do we let these people bother a pastor, or any other working part of the body of Christ? We want to be nice and not hurt their feelings; but in doing so, we let them hurt others. More importantly, we let them do Satan's work by hindering God's work and God's people. These people simply wear us out. Somehow, it becomes about who helped start the church. Who has been there the longest? Who puts in the money, along with all the other meaningless factors, instead of maturity and servanthood for Christ. When we become mature in Christ, we find, first of all, the true realization of how very unimportant and unworthy we are.

Now we all know there are some of us that are really good, and need to be directing, guiding, and managing those that are much less fortunate. It is wonderful that God gifted us so richly, and gave us the understanding to know how good we are. If you have any thought of how great and good you are, please leave your pastor and church alone! With this understanding, we can truly praise God for allowing such sinners as we are to even be worthy of cleaning the church restrooms. When we understand how much of an honor it is to serve in any capacity, we are starting to mature in Christ. Maturity in Jesus is the life of a servant. Any other attitude than this is not acceptable in serving God's people and God's pastors. This includes pastors!

> And whosoever will be chief among you, let him be your servant: Even as the Son of man came not to be ministered unto, but to minister, and to give His life a ransom for many.
> —MATTHEW 20:27–28

And he sat down, and called the twelve, and saith unto them, If any man desire to be first, the same shall be last of all, and servant of all.

—MARK 9:35

And whosoever of you will be the chiefest, shall be servant of all. For even the Son of man came not to be ministered unto, but to minister, and to give his life a ransom for many.

—MARK 10:44–45

Blessed is that servant, whom his lord when he cometh shall find so doing.

—LUKE 12:43

Jesus was very clear on how to serve in His kingdom, being meticulous in His examples of how we are to be and act. Jesus' way is different than the world's way. It even conflicts with the world's methods for us to succeed in our carnal jobs. However, the servants of the churches will be the only successful pastoral farmers. The self-appointed bosses, critics, and those who tell us how to do it, but have never done it themselves. Stop them, it's not about them. They must never be a part of any process of a young pastor's life and ministry.

Prune these people before they affect any new young pastor. Prune away these encumbrances along with the draining process of having to deal with these destructive types. If we stop them from stealing valuable time and resources, we can save many young pastors.

We must understand that we, the world, and God all need the pastors. We will never run out of people with big mouths. They can weaken the whole body of Christ, as well as your pastor. If you and your church are in the mind-set that these people have done so much for the church that they need to be allowed the liberty of directing, guiding, and getting their way with the pastor, look closely and pray for a discerning spirit.

The truth is, more than likely, you're doing more for Satan than for God by keeping these people in influential positions in the church! If you have a good seedling pastor, he or she will either die or will soon move. It is really important we understand that some of these people simply do not know better, and they feel they are doing what is right. We must show them the right way, God's way, firmly but in love. We should correct ourselves before God corrects us. Everyone who wants to be the head, or control the head, is not of God. Please understand that our pastors are called by God and not by man. They are to work for God and not man. We should know that our God is a jealous God.

What do we think happens when we try to take His place and destroy His chosen vessels? They are God's chosen vessels, and if anyone is trying to choose the direction and messages that are coming from the pulpit, they are working for Satan. Prune back severely in this area. It can never be acceptable, not even for a short time. This is a disease straight from hell and is highly contagious. Prune deep, but as always prune in *love*.

I would like for everyone to reflect here. How many decisions for a church are made by a handful of people who haven't been on their knees for a long time, if ever? Many decisions are based on man-made doctrine or some other rules made by men and women. No matter how good the intentions, many times they are contrary to God's Word and His will. We really must get a grasp on reality. The body of Christ is to be like a business—a business that hears from God, that is. Businesses have to produce and will spend time in product development to remain in operation. Look at how many great things were accomplished by people in the Bible who started out looking incapable but did mighty and great things by the hand of God. Pastors need to take time to grow and to develop. We even miss the mark sometimes when God may be doing a work in a pastor, perhaps establishing faith and trust in Him, and then we interfere by assisting him with worldly advice and management skills. Without any knowledge from God and without hearing from God, worldly decisions are made. We think we need to jump in, in front of God, not in obedience, but in our own judgment.

So many churches are in waste. They produce virtually no fruit, even though their decisions are based on the very best intentions and great, but worldly, management skills. These are good people trying their best to do what is right. Many times the result is completely missing God's plan and the greatness that was destined to be from it! Decision makers must be in prayer, fasting, and always be extremely well grounded in the Word of God. Understand this please: without praying, fasting, and having God's Word in us, we will miss the place where God wants us to be! The very best intentions of many will not equal one little direction from God. If you do not know from God what you are personally to do and what God's will is for your particular church, please find out before ever making a decision concerning a pastor or church.

Churches of every denomination really need to get this right. If you think things are not wrong now, that we as a Church have not missed God, you need to explain why the world is serving Satan instead of God. It is not right, and we all must be about getting it right. Today there are many schools turning out ministers and pastors. Some of these schools have zeal, but are only offering an education designed after the school's heart and not God's heart. What is really being produced is a hybrid. A hybrid is a cross between two species. Man is trying to cross his will with the will of God. Only God is capable of manifesting Himself in man. A hybrid will not produce the fruit God intended. It has, however, been very successful because man-made hybrids produced the fruit man desired, not what God desired.

This is the way of many of the churches we see today. They advertise "church your way," "contemporary this and modern that." Some even guarantee that you will be in and out in thirty minutes. If God wanted to show up, He would have to do so by an appointment or a committee meeting. Man wants church his way and on his terms. Look at the phone book again. Simply ask yourself, how many churches and how many divisions did Jesus establish in His church? In fact, if we study Jesus' teachings, he never had one good word to say about religion or its institutions. He condemned them and clearly stated that they were not of God. (See John 8:42–45.)

If your church is a "religious" place of worship, God is not there. I believe most church members in these churches know this and understand the real position of their church; but because of the difficulty they have with confrontation, they have not done anything about it. Sometimes the problem seems too big and has just plain gone on for too long. We must understand and trust that when we strive to get it God's way, and not ours, God will show up and do His part. Why is it so hard for us to trust in God? We don't even seem to trust Him with His own Word in His own house! Let's get on God's side and be right in the middle of His will.

> If any man among you seems to be religious, and bridleth not his tongue, but deceiveth his own heart, this man's religion is vain. Pure religion and undefiled before God and the Father is this, To visit the fatherless and widows in their affliction, and to keep himself unspotted from the world.
> —JAMES 1:26–27

We must ask and keep asking ourselves, does my religion and my denomination line up with the Word of God? There are many churches full of good programs and great ideas. They are busy going about the deeds and needs of the church but have never fulfilled one Word of Jesus. We must ask, am I zealous about a doctrine of a church, or am I zealous about God and God's will for my life? When was the last time we prayed to be used as a blessing to someone, instead of asking for a blessing? I have been in a church that was all about itself. In fact, I matured greatly there and was fed the Word of God. There were some good things done there and it was all done with the best of intentions, however more time and money was always spent for programs that did more entertaining than ministering. Evangelism and missions were basically nonexistent. These types of churches will never fulfill God's plan.

> Beware of the scribes, which desire to walk in long robes, and love greetings in the markets, and the highest seats in the synagogues, and the chief rooms at feasts; which devour widows' houses, and for a shew make long prayers: the same shall receive greater damnation.
> —LUKE 20:46–47

Do not grow a hybrid or get one that is already grown. Only God creates a pastor. Let me say that again—only God can create a pastor. No one can make one and no one can become one unless they are called by God. We can only provide the needed environment and meet the nutritional needs required for pastors to grow.

Run and run fast from any hybrid pastors and the churches they are producing. They are designed and produced by man and not by God. Their fruit will be pleasing to man, but not to God. They will work hard. They will look good. They will sound good, and most of all, their teaching will deceive many in the body of Christ. A hybrid will look like an apple, and may taste like an apple, but it is not an apple.

> For such are false apostles, deceitful workers, transforming themselves into the apostles of Christ. And no marvel; for Satan himself is transformed into an angel of light. Therefore it is no great thing if his ministers also be transformed as the ministers of righteousness; whose end shall be according to their works.
> —2 CORINTHIANS 11:13–15

I have said many times and will keep on saying, "Satan is good, very good at what he does." Come on church, let us wake up and get this! There are millions being deceived into false salvation, a false Christian lifestyle, and they do not even realize their situation. They need real godly pastors raised up proclaiming the truth before it is too late for them.

> For many deceivers are entered into the world, who confess not that Jesus Christ is come in the flesh. This is a deceiver and an antichrist.
> —2 JOHN 1:7

Do you have friends and fellow workers who say, "Well, I'm not sure Jesus is real, or He was real but He was just another prophet"? Maybe these are neighbors or relatives of yours who deny Jesus is the Christ. Look at what God has to say about these people: they are of the Antichrist. Remember that the next time you invite someone into your house. Can we let Satan into our home, or allow him to influence our children by something this simple and seemingly so innocent? You better know we can!

> Ye are of your father the devil, and the lusts of your father ye will do. He was a murderer from the beginning, and abode not in the

truth, because there is no truth in him. When he speaketh a lie, he speaketh of his own: for he is a liar, and the father of it.

—JOHN 8:44

Today this is so very true. Take a look at the fastest growing religions. They are not of God because they do not put Jesus as their Lord and Savior. There is one head of the church, and He will come for His Church, His bride. I hope everyone who reads this book will understand that with the very best of intentions, without even an idea of what we may have done, we can grow or transplant Satan into our churches, our lives, and our homes. We must be careful, very careful of which tree we grow, transplant, or even eat from. There are literally millions every Sunday being fed worldly and corrupt lies that have been purposely designed to deceive them. We must never allow ourselves to be fed from a hybrid. Satan started this whole mess by fooling us with the wrong tree and fruit. Eve was told then, "Ye shall not surely die." We know that was a lie, and so are Satan's words today a lie. When are we going to get this right? God help us! We have been told by God's own Word, we have been repeatedly told by prophets, yet we still listen to Satan. I am so thankful that I will be receiving what Jesus did for me instead of what I deserve.

> Even so every good tree bringeth forth good fruit; but a corrupt tree bringeth forth evil fruit. A good tree cannot bring forth evil fruit, neither can a corrupt tree bring forth good fruit. Every tree that bringeth not forth good fruit is hewn down, and cast into the fire. Wherefore by their fruits ye shall know them.
>
> —MATTHEW 7:17–20

> He that hath an ear, let him hear what the Spirit saith unto the churches; To him that overcometh will I give to eat of the tree of life, which is in the midst of the paradise of God.
>
> —REVELATION 2:7

The body of Christ must always be reviewing our fruit. What are we and our church producing—fruit pleasing to man or to God? If your pastor is preaching to "tickle their ears," they are going to "feel good" all the way to hell. This is serious business. We are either doing God's work or Satan's. The evidence will be in the fruit.

We are to be growing pastors to head the church, Jesus' church. I'm going to step on some of those religious toes here. Beware if you grow, plant, or transplant a pastor who is more of a man of your particular church doctrine than he is a man of God who promotes the gospel of Jesus Christ. This kind of pastor can only produce doctrinal fruit. It will not be godly fruit.

> Be not deceived; God is not mocked: for whatsoever a man soweth, that shall he also reap. For he that soweth to his flesh shall of the flesh reap corruption; but he that soweth to the Spirit shall of the Spirit reap life everlasting. And let us not be weary in well doing: for in due season we shall reap, if we faint not.
> —GALATIANS 6:7–9

If you want a pastor who is more of your church teaching and following your church doctrine, I beg you to pray and seek God. I do not want to hurt your feelings, but I would have a sincere doubt that you are truly saved. Your church and all your church doctrine cannot save you. We must be growing pastors who will serve God's will and preach God's Word, caring not for man-made, Satan-influenced doctrine. These pastors are to grow Jesus' church, not a man-made church. There is nothing wrong with belonging to a denomination. In fact, many denominations with considerable numbers of churches and larger memberships should be stronger, and their power to influence should be greater, to fulfill God's purpose and will. However, when the denominations are put above God, their creeds and rules above the Word of God, and their needs and ambitions before the kingdom of God, it is wrong. In many cases, this is the reality. It was not purposed to be, but just became that way over time. Every church needs to examine itself. And it needs to judge itself according to what the Word of God says and throw out all that man has added over time.

We are running out of time, so please hear this. All, and I do mean all, of our churches have been attacked by Satan. We all have been deceived to some extent and to some degree. Satan is your enemy, as well as God's enemy!

> Ye adulterers and adulteresses, know ye not that the friendship of the world is enmity with God? whosoever therefore will be a friend of the world is the enemy of God. Do ye think that the scripture saith in vain, The spirit that dwelleth in us lusteth to envy? But he giveth more grace. Wherefore he saith, God resisteth the proud, but giveth grace unto the humble. Submit yourselves therefore to God. Resist the devil, and he will flee from you. Draw nigh to God, and he will draw nigh to you. Cleanse your hands, ye sinners; and purify your hearts, ye double minded.
>
> —JAMES 4:4–8

We must not be a part of growing a minister of Satan. We think this could not happen in our church, right? Satan could not possibly be in any church, and every other church is wrong but ours, right? We have declared and decreed. We have the truth, and bless God, we are the only denomination so far to get it right. Can we all be this stupid? It appears that for the most part the answer is *yes!* It is time we join as brothers and sisters of Christ. It is time that each one of us stops being whatever denomination we are and simply be a son or daughter of God. Before all things, above all things, and more important than all things, we must be Jesus!. We must start agreeing and working together on all the things that we do agree on and not let our differences divide.

It is time we come together in understanding that only Satan would cause division and disunity in the body of Christ. As Scripture reminds us, it is Satan who steals, kills, and destroys: "The thief cometh not, but for to steal, and to kill, and to destroy: I am come that they might have life, and that they might have it more abundantly" (John 10:10).

Christians have allowed Satan to divide the church. The truth is very plain and we need to understand the real meaning to the body of Christ.

> Now concerning spiritual gifts, brethren, I would not have you ignorant. Ye know that ye were Gentiles, carried away unto these dumb idols, even as ye were led. Wherefore I give you to understand, that no man speaking by the Spirit of God calleth Jesus accursed: and that no man can say that Jesus is the Lord,

but by the Holy Ghost. Now there are diversities of gifts, but the same Spirit. And there are differences of administrations, but the same Lord. And there are diversities of operations, but it is the same God which worketh all in all. But the manifestation of the Spirit is given to every man to profit withal. For to one is given by the Spirit the word of wisdom; to another the word of knowledge by the same Spirit; To another faith by the same Spirit; to another the gifts of healing by the same Spirit; To another the working of miracles; to another prophecy; to another discerning of spirits; to another divers kinds of tongues; to another the interpretation of tongues: But all these worketh that one and the selfsame Spirit, dividing to every man severally as he will. For as the body is one, and hath many members, and all the members of that one body, being many, are one body: so also is Christ. For by one Spirit are we all baptized into one body, whether we be Jews or Gentiles, whether we be bond or free; and have been all made to drink into one Spirit. For the body is not one member, but many. If the foot shall say, Because I am not the hand, I am not of the body; is it therefore not of the body? And if the ear shall say, Because I am not the eye, I am not of the body; is it therefore not of the body? If the whole body were an eye, where were the hearing? If the whole were hearing, where were the smelling? But now hath God set the members every one of them in the body, as it hath pleased him. And if they were all one member, where were the body? But now are they many members, yet but one body.

—1 CORINTHIANS 12:1–20

Let us look at this in, what may be, a new light for some of us. This is one of the most important parts of this book. Please take a moment and pray. Ask God to share with you by revealing His Word and His meaning to you. God will reveal His Word to us. This verse starts off with Paul telling us that he does not want us to be ignorant of spiritual gifts. It has really amazed me how something that God's Word has called spiritual gifts, gifts of the Holy Ghost, and what Jesus said would be power, has so divided us. We know God did not intend for us to be divided.

> But ye shall receive power, after that the Holy Ghost is come
> upon you: and ye shall be witnesses unto me both in Jerusalem,
> and in all Judaea, and in Samaria, and unto the uttermost part
> of the earth.
>
> —ACTS 1:8

Many believe this was for a time long ago, for the early church, and not needed now. Many others believe this is for the church today. I'm not going to allow this to cause distraction from the topic of this book. It has always been our human understanding that one side must be wrong. We can most assuredly agree we won't agree which side is wrong. I will discuss this topic later in this book. I do believe both sides are wrong in allowing this to divide the body of Christ.

Would it be possible to even accept that if there is power from God we need it badly? Viewing the condition of our churches, our country, and our world, if it is power for today, we need to learn to use that power. If it is a gift from God, how do we get such a gift? We must search God's Word—where we will find it. God gave us His Word, the Bible, to guide us, so let's review in prayer and unity what it says.

If we really study these gifts, as they are listed in 1 Corinthians 12:8–10, we will see there are nine different and separate gifts. It states clearly that these gifts are given some to one and some to another. The gifts are wisdom, knowledge, faith, healing, miracles, prophecy, discerning of spirits, diverse kind of tongues, and interpretation of tongues. It is evident to me that almost every blood-bought church believes in, needs, wants, and, in some form, uses the first seven of the nine. Every true church seeks from God wisdom, knowledge, faith, healing, miracles, prophecy, and discernment. Most families are not even in agreement 78 percent of the time, yet we have allowed this to be a huge division of the church body. Both sides need to understand God's position on unity and become unified. Quit being in opposition. Quit being someone who has a set position and let us all be a part of the body of Christ.

> Behold, how good and how pleasant it is for brethren to dwell
> together in unity! It is like the precious ointment upon the head,

that ran down upon the beard, even Aaron's beard: that went down to the skirts of his garments; As the dew of Hermon, and as the dew that descended upon the mountains of Zion: for there the LORD commanded the blessing, even life for evermore.

—PSALM 133

Now let us really look at 1 Corinthians 12:12. Here is an important part: all members are of one body, so also is Christ. We all agree Jesus is going to return, and we all know He's coming for *one* church, without spot or wrinkle. (See Ephesians 5:27.) Let us become one church, loving our brothers and sisters in Christ. Heaven forbid in the end, at that "twinkling of an eye," we might find out that the denomination down the street was right—and we were wrong! We must understand that the most learned and religious men giving full-time service to God completely missed Jesus, and furthered Satan's agenda and not God's. We read these events in the Bible and wonder how they were ever a part of crucifying Jesus. How are we a part of allowing the greatest nation on earth to kill five thousand babies today? What did we do when they took prayer out of school? Yet we have the audacity to take a firm dogmatic stand on a difference of an interpretation and divide the church. The truth is, not much had changed between Adam and Jesus, and not much has changed since Jesus and today. Let us never be too sure of ourselves, let us be sure of God and God's Word. Can we understand the importance of love, unity, and obedience to God? Do we understand where we are at in division and discord?

Studying 1 Corinthians 12:18, we must acknowledge that in speaking of the gifts and the body (Jesus' church), it says, "God set the members, every one of them in the body, *as it hath pleased him*" (emphasis added). I truly hope we can start coming together in understanding that we, individually, are a part of His body. Every true church of believers is purchased with the blood of our Christ and is a part, as it pleases God. I know one thing for sure, it is not going to be a doctrine or denominational interpretation that pleases God. Rather, it is going to be the condition of our hearts and our place in His Son's body that counts. How is your heart? What is your place? These are two important questions that we all must be asking ourselves on a regular basis.

> Now ye are the body of Christ, and members in particular. And God hath set some in the church, first apostles, secondarily prophets, thirdly teachers, after that miracles, then gifts of healings, helps, governments, diversities of tongues.
>
> —1 CORINTHIANS 12:27–28

If we are a part, and the church down the street is a part, and both are placed there by God, and it pleases God—but we can't or won't work together to expand the kingdom of God—then we must ask ourselves: where do we stand with God and God's plan? The driest, most fundamentalist church, and the most charismatic, Pentecostal church are a part of the body. Get over it and understand it pleases God.

Prune away divisional church doctrine, church isolation, human pride, and those who believe they are the only right ones. The truth is, we all have probably missed more than we have got right, and have caused many to leave our churches lost and confused in the process. Do we as a church realize how many will not come to a church because of the actions and attitudes of those in the church? Prune so new growth will be of God. If we prune well, very well, and begin with ourselves, we will be able to have what God grows. We must seek growth from God, not man. We will then be able to be and do what God intends for us, our pastors, and Jesus' churches when we are truly His branches.

> I am the true vine, and my Father is the husbandman. Every branch in me that beareth not fruit he taketh away: and every branch that beareth fruit, he purgeth it, that it may bring forth more fruit. Now ye are clean through the word which I have spoken unto you.
>
> —JOHN 15:1–3

> Praising God, and having favour with all the people. And the Lord added to the church daily such as should be saved.
>
> —ACTS 2:47

Let us understand the following verse as it so applies to us as well as the Jews, which I pray you are praying for. If you and your church are not praying for Israel, you are not in God's will. Please do not miss this.

And they also, if they abide not still in unbelief, shall be grafted in: for God is able to graff them in again. For if thou wert cut out of the olive tree which is wild by nature, and wert grafted contrary to nature into a good olive tree: how much more shall these, which be the natural branches, be grafted into their own olive tree?

—ROMANS 11:23–24

Pastor-pruning is where we can help our pastors cut away the old so new will grow. One of the biggest helps we can provide is simply by allowing and encouraging. I have tried to promote several joint efforts among area churches. It will seldom happen. On the other hand, in the secular world, car lots come together for the good of themselves and have joint sales events together. Similarly, many nightclubs and bars get together to promote events. Satan's crews work well together, but the churches can't or won't, and it is sad. This lack of unity among churches is wrong and it needs to stop. In truth, most pastors are afraid they will lose some of their sheep to another pastor if they join together. They do not want to mix flocks.

First and foremost, the sheep do not belong to the pastor. They are Jesus' sheep. God will add to the church as He sees fit, not as the pastors see fit. But churches must understand that the underlying problem is if some of the flock leaves, everyone blames the pastor. Grow up, go about God's work, and quit looking at numbers and blaming each other. We must have faith that God is in control. We are simply to be busy about God's work. God's part is to bless the church. It is our lack, not the pastor's. We must grow a pastor to have freedom to do God's will and not our will. If we really want a great church with a great pastor, we have to grow one God's way. We can do this by providing the needed environment for God to do the growing. Then and only then will your church be truly Jesus' church and your pastor, God's pastor.

Secondly, we really need to get real. There are times that God moves people. There are also times when people move themselves for a variety of reasons. If someone finds there is another church or pastor of which they want to be a part, it is probably for the best. They may really grow and do more to help the kingdom of God having their needs met elsewhere. They had to be missing something where they were. People who feel this way usually end up causing strife and trouble. By them moving on, the trouble has been eliminated. When we put it in the light of what is always best or the kingdom of God, and not for ourselves personally or our church, we are becoming more like Jesus. Many of us will never get to this place, but praise God some will.

Where there is light, darkness cannot stand. We must achieve a place in God where the light of God is shining so brightly in us and our churches that all can see God. It is in this place that Satan, as darkness, must leave; for he cannot remain where there is light. We must be in subjection to God's Word and will, ready at all times to be in the presence of our Savior, our King, our Lord, Jesus the Christ.

> Therefore as the church is subject unto Christ, so let the wives be to their own husbands in every thing. Husbands, love your wives, even as Christ also loved the church, and gave himself for it; That he might sanctify and cleanse it with the washing of water by the word, That he might present it to himself a glorious church, not having spot, or wrinkle, or any such thing; but that it should be holy and without blemish.
>
> —EPHESIANS 5:24–27

To Jesus, the church was so important that He referred to it as His bride. We must understand the importance of this. A bride becomes intimate with the groom and they have a relationship. When it is done in God's will, it is also a blood covenant. This relationship is to be so changing that they become one. We must be striving for that kind of a relationship with our Groom, Jesus! We are to be His church! We are not to have spot, or wrinkle, or any such thing and we must be holy without blemish. We must ask ourselves continually, "Is this our church or Jesus'? Is it like Jesus describes?" More important than anything else, we need to pray, "God, in Jesus' name, please reveal to me every spot or wrinkle that is in me or because of me." The day we think all of the problems are only in others and not in us, we are worthless to our pastor, to ourselves, and to God. We then become prime candidates to do Satan's work.

And I John saw the holy city, new Jerusalem, coming down from God out of heaven, prepared as a bride adorned for her husband. And I heard a great voice out of heaven saying, Behold, the tabernacle of God is with men, and he will dwell with them, and they shall be his people, and God himself shall be with them, and be their God.

—REVELATION 21:2–3

And there came unto me one of the seven angels which had the seven vials full of the seven last plagues, and talked with me, saying, Come hither, I will shew thee the bride, the Lamb's wife. And he carried me away in the spirit to a great and high mountain, and shewed me that great city, the holy Jerusalem, descending out of heaven from God.

—REVELATION 21:9–10

Blessed are they that do his commandments, that they may have right to the tree of life, and may enter in through the gates into the city. For without are dogs, and sorcerers, and whoremongers, and murderers, and idolaters, and whosoever loveth and maketh a lie. I Jesus have sent mine angel to testify unto you these things in the churches. I am the root and the offspring of David, and the bright and morning star. And the Spirit and the bride say, Come. And let him that heareth say, Come. And let him that is athirst come. And whosoever will, let him take the water of life freely. For I testify unto every man that heareth the words of the prophecy of this book, If any man shall add unto these things, God shall add unto him the plagues that are written in this book: And if any man shall take away from the words of the book of this prophecy, God shall take away his part out of the book of life, and out of the holy city, and from the things which are written in this book. He which testifieth these things saith, Surely I come quickly. Amen. Even so, come, Lord Jesus. The grace of our Lord Jesus Christ be with you all. Amen.

—REVELATION 22:14–21

This is the Book of Revelation, which was written by John, the one the Master loved. To appreciate this book, one must study the life of John. I will not present a study here, except to say that John was not only boiled in oil, but was boiled more than once, and then exiled to the island of Patmos. Like many of those who were martyrs for the gospel of Jesus, John paid a great price. He, under the inspiration of God, in the very presence of the resurrected living Jesus, said these words to us. Let us not forget them:

> Blessed is he that readeth, and they that hear the words of this prophecy, and keep those things which are written therein: for the time is at hand.
>
> —REVELATION 1:3

Let's look at the importance of that little seed you're planting. First and foremost, we must be sure it is of God and not of Satan. Pastors must be grown in the Word of God with nothing added and nothing removed. We must understand that anything more or less is of Satan and will be about Satan's work and not God's work.

> And if any man shall take away from the words of the book of this prophecy, God shall take away his part out of the book of life, and out of the holy city, and from the things which are written in this book.
>
> —REVELATION 22:19

We must not be a part of anything contrary to the Word of God. We, for sure, don't want to be a part of adding to or taking away from God's Word and His works. Our pastors are certainly part of God's work. They are trying to make a vessel of God follow some man-made doctrine, no matter how old, or how well-meaning, and for what purpose. If God's Word is not set up to be followed, then we will find ourselves against God. Sometimes this requires hard choices that only can be made in the maturity of Jesus, not by the maturity of a church.

> And he spake to them a parable; Behold the fig tree, and all the trees; When they now shoot forth, ye see and know of your own selves that summer is now nigh at hand. So likewise ye, when ye see these things come to pass, know ye that the kingdom of God is nigh at hand. Verily I say unto you, This generation shall not pass away, till all be fulfilled. Heaven and earth shall pass away:

but my words shall not pass away. And take heed to yourselves, lest at any time your hearts be overcharged with surfeiting, and drunkenness, and cares of this life, and so that day come upon you unawares. For as a snare shall it come on all them that dwell on the face of the whole earth. Watch ye therefore, and pray always, that ye may be accounted worthy to escape all these things that shall come to pass, and to stand before the Son of man.

—LUKE 21:29-36

We, as a body of Christ in America, have allowed ourselves to be changed, little by little. We have become accepting of the unacceptable. In review of the last fifteen years of our country's history, we simply have abandoned God's Word. Prostitution is now legal in some states and ignored in most. Abortion is legal. Five thousand babies die every day. In fact, during this very day, in which you are reading this book in this country five thousand innocent babies are murdered. It has become about the rights of worldly men and women and not about the will of God. Homosexuality now fights to have "rights." We even have homosexuals as priests. Contrary to the beliefs of some, these churches are not serving God. In fact, they and everyone who supports them in any way is serving Satan. (See 1 Corinthians 6:9.)

Good people, in fact some of the best, had to make a really hard choice. Should they support a church of which they were a part and loved so much, or should they support God? These are hard, very hard choices, and we need to be in prayer for them. There is a hard rule that I follow. This is simply a "Ron Rule" and not a scriptural one, but if something has Satan in it, then God's not in it. The Spirit of light will not be where the spirit of darkness is. Homosexuality and gay or lesbian priests are of Satan, God is not in it. Do not support it. How many young children have been molested in churches, physically, in the very building that is to be God's house of prayer? How many of those cases were either ignored or swept under the carpet, because the church's people did not know the full truth or what to do about it?

We must understand that now is the time to pray for these churches and support them to repent and get Satan out of the church. Our brothers and sisters need our support, not our scorn. Many of these churches are now filing bankruptcy. If you do not think Satan is in the churches, you are wrong. When a church, any church, opens a door to a man-made doctrine, Satan comes in faster than he fell from heaven, which was as quick as lightning. It's so important to be sure that we are growing a pastor of God. Before planting, pray, pray, and then pray some more. God will move. God will always, and I mean always, confirm His Word. Let us bring Jesus' bride together in holiness and righteousness. One body, pure in thoughts, deeds, and hearts.

Wow, we spent a lot of time on that seed, but now we are going to plant a seed, and it will be of God. Next, we need to know what kind of godly apple we are going to plant. As there are a variety of apples for a variety of uses, so it goes for pastors. I love green, sour apples with a lot of salt, but most would not like the pie they would make. In an extreme analogy, the very best godly white American seedling pastor, put in the best mostly Hispanic church and neighborhood, would probably fail miserably. Would it be the pastor's fault? No. Does it mean the church is at fault? No, only in their choice of seed or "tree" to grow. That pastor would not understand all the cultural issues of his sheep and might have to overcome language barriers.

We all know and can thank God that many of these issues have been torn down. We can and should worship God with all people. It would be just as difficult to take a pastor from New York City and put him or her in a farming community in the Deep South. He would be out of place. Yes, he might grow very slowly and might produce fruit, but perhaps not much fruit. We could take a charismatic Holy Spirit-filled pastor, doing a great job, and put him in a more traditional, conservative setting and he or she would not be accepted. We then could take the same successful pastor with the same Word of God to a different location and have drastically different results. These decisions must be made with prayer and fasting. We must get to where pastors are serving where they are called by God, not to where man wants them. It can't even be about where the pastor wants to be. It always must be about God's plan.

We have half-full churches blocks apart in most towns in the United States, yet whole nations are still lost. Pastors are not going into trouble zones. Can we believe that many of these pastors are not called to the inner city slums to break the cycle of poverty or to reach the lost? Or can we believe that many are not called to Africa, Russia, India, Iraq, and other devastated countries in these last days? Can we believe these are God's plans? Can we believe these are all God's churches and none of these pastors were called to go to any of these countries? Again, these are really hard choices!

We must be sure we are growing God's pastors, full of God's Word and walking in His wisdom and knowledge, not man's. A word of advice to churches that are seeking pastors, and to pastors seeking churches: people are not changed by pastors and pastors are not changed by churches. Only God changes people as well as pastors. We must have the right tree to produce the right fruit in the right conditions. Speaking to young pastors, and wannabees, and "going-to-bees": you have a very important responsibility to be sure you're in the right place!

Caution, pastors, beware that you are not just taking it for granted that you're not one of those that is being deceived. Don't be fooled into thinking that you can't be deceived into being trained as a minister of Satan. You must personally be responsible for making sure that you and your ministry line up with and stand only for the Word of God. If you can't do that, then get out of the ministry. Satan, for sure, will get hold of you!

If you do not, or won't allow God and God's Word to guide and teach you, you'll be worthless to God! Trust in God or everything else will fail you and the people you are to serve. Know, I mean really know, your master. Is Jesus really the Lord of your life? Is the fruit you're producing bearing witness to God? Every pastor, teacher, and church worker of every kind must understand they will be held to a higher standard.

> But have renounced the hidden things of dishonesty, not walking in craftiness, nor handling the word of God deceitfully; but by manifestation of the truth commending ourselves to every man's conscience in the sight of God.
>
> —2 CORINTHIANS 4:2

> Study to shew thyself approved unto God, a workman that needeth not to be ashamed, rightly dividing the word of truth.
>
> —2 TIMOTHY 2:15

When we as teachers, preachers, pastors, and ministers of God's Word stand before the judgment bar of Christ, as we all must, the requirements will be much higher, and require much more. We are charged with knowing the truth and must understand we have to do better! We are to be servants of the one and only most high God. God's Word will stand forever, so we must be centered in it.

> Heaven and earth shall pass away, but my words shall not pass away.
>
> —MATTHEW 24:35

Speaking incorrectly or misusing God's Word is a ticket straight to hell. I believe there are many men and women in churches, and on television and radio today, that make a living using God's Word for their own benefit. I believe that not only will they literally burn in hell, but, I believe the flames will be hotter and higher. Pray for these people that the conviction of almighty God will fall on them before it's too late.

> And that servant, which knew his lord's will, and prepared not himself, neither did according to his will, shall be beaten with many stripes. But he that knew not, and did commit things worthy of stripes, shall be beaten with few stripes. For unto whomsoever much is given, of him shall be much required: and to whom men have committed much, of him they will ask the more.
>
> —LUKE 12:47–48

There are two areas of great concern here: the pastors who simply are mistaken, and the pastors who know better, but have fallen to worldly lust, money, pride, fame, and a self-serving spirit. Since this chapter is on growing a pastor from seed, we are going to speak only of the mistaken young pastors. They are going to make mistakes—the more work they do, the more mistakes they will make. This is where every young pastor needs the headship of an older experienced pastor. If you're growing a pastor from seed, get a mature, godly pastor to oversee, advise, and mentor. Godly pastors will produce godly pastors by their tutoring, mentoring, and imparting of knowledge.

The last thing a young pastor needs is a bunch of critics who find pleasure in pointing out mistakes. This is not to say that we should not bring to attention an area that we think is in error. It should, however, be done in humility and with love. Before you start correcting, please remember the words Jesus spoke:

> And why beholdest thou the mote that is in thy brother's eye, but considerest not the beam that is in thine own eye? Or how wilt thou say to thy brother, Let me pull out the mote out of thine eye; and, behold, a beam is in thine own eye? Thou hypocrite, first cast out the beam out of thine own eye; and then shalt thou see clearly to cast out the mote out of thy brother's eye.
>
> —MATTHEW 7:3–5

Chapter Three

TWIGS THAT
MAKE MIGHTY TREES

The analogy of a tree and a pastor is really so real to life. In the last chapter, we discussed growing a pastor from a seed. In this chapter, we will discuss growing a pastor that is already a tree, howbeit a small one. The comparison of a tree to man was used several times by God; if it works for Him, it works for me. Besides, it is so true how similarly a tree grows to how we, and our pastors, are to grow. God really did use the same principal to grow both.

The "young tree" pastor has some roots and some growth of leaves and branches. He or she still has not produced any fruit but will start the process of blossoming. We must have blossoms before fruit. As the limbs begin to grow and before the blossoms spring forth is the time of pruning. Here is the deciding point; the point that will decide which fruit will be produced and how the tree will be shaped. Some trees will need little or no pruning, some will need minor pruning, and some will literally have to be cut back to the trunk, being completely reshaped. If pruned correctly and according to God's Word, all sprigs will grow into godly trees. Normally, the biggest problem for this point in a pastor's growth is the environment. Like all living

51

creatures, pastoral growth is affected by the growing conditions. Circumstances that are too wet or too dry, too hot or too cold will create undesirable trees. The worst condition by far, however, is an environment that is too dark. The most severe problem that causes spiritual abnormality is not enough light—spiritual light.

> Then spake Jesus again unto them, saying, I am the light of the world: he that followeth me shall not walk in darkness, but shall have the light of life.
>
> —JOHN 8:12

> Take heed therefore that the light which is in thee be not darkness. If thy whole body therefore be full of light, having no part dark, the whole shall be full of light, as when the bright shining of a candle doth give thee light.
>
> —LUKE 11:35–36

Now is when the tree must have the light of Jesus. These real pastoral trees, that will become capable of producing kingdom fruits, must be continually receiving the real light before they can produce anything for God or receive anything from God. When I state that many young pastors do not receive this godly light at the most critical time in their growth, and that they never produce the fruit God had ordained for their ministries, most people will not believe me. It is true and we need to recognize the problem and provide the solution. Many young pastors are faced with financial burdens, family responsibilities, as well as needing to meet the requirements of many other classes and courses to graduate from school. The truth is many have little time to be in the presence of Christ on a continual basis. The result of this is evident by their growth and the fruit they produce. It is not their fault. They are doing their best. The question is, are we doing our best for them?

Our government and many large corporations spend millions of dollars to help train Olympic athletes. Their commitment to the athlete is to be esteemed. The fruition of their commitment and their resources are just accomplishments that last for a few moments every four years. How is it that the men and women of God, whose contributions will last for all eternity, must struggle? Where are the corporations that support athletes that run the continual race for God, competing against Satan everyday? Every gold medal ever won will pass away, but the heavenly rewards will last for an eternity. Would it not be great to see some large corporations catch on to this knowledge and reward program? Where are the priorities of our churches and each and every one of us individually? Where are we going to get the men and women of God who will encourage, educate, and lead us to godly achievements in these last days?

What are the churches doing to raise up pastors? We all need to take a closer look and be prepared to do our part. It's important we know our responsibilities as well as those of the young pastors we are trying to grow. We are all at fault and need to really look at ourselves and our church's fundamental mentality. We must start with the realization that man's flesh will always get it wrong. We are of the sick and perverse generation. We see wonderful and beautiful buildings with many more programs of all types, but no money to send the youth to seminary. Not only is this a very sad condition, but also there are several churches that fund themselves as a means of making money by teaching how to spread the gospel. Know this! They missed the, "Freely I have received and freely I give," part of the Bible. (See Matthew 10:8.) I am so thankful Jesus didn't charge us for His knowledge and understanding. You do not want a pastor raised up in a school, or a church, who was raised up just to raise money. Please understand there are denominational seminaries that charge for schooling, and most try to do an honorable work. It is the Reverend Joe Blow that has been issued some "fly by night" seminary license that anyone can purchase—that is the problem.

> He spake also this parable; A certain man had a fig tree planted in his vineyard; and he came and sought fruit thereon, and found none. Then said he unto the dresser of his vineyard, Behold, these three years I come seeking fruit on this fig tree, and find none: cut it down; why cumbereth it the ground? And he answering said unto him, Lord, let it alone this year also, till I shall dig about it, and dung it: And if it bear fruit, well: and if not, then after that thou shalt cut it down.
>
> —LUKE 13:6–9

53

The dresser (keeper, tender) of this tree has an obligation as well as an opportunity to assist the tree to bear fruit. He is to dig (cultivate) and dung (fertilize) the tree. God's Word clearly tells the church body what its responsibility is toward pastors at all times in a pastor's life. It is clear that a tree not bearing fruit is unacceptable. There are to be dressers in the body of Christ. We are to be a part, and must do our part, but we also must not interfere with God's part or the pastor's part. There are some very important items here, and we should make sure we understand. Not bearing fruit is unacceptable. We have a responsible part in the fruit-bearing process. The pastor has his or her part of the process. God has a part in the process. We cannot, nor can we ever, try to do the pastor's part, and certainly not God's part.

As important to this tree's growth and life as digging and dunging were, we must understand that the light of God is more important. We must ensure that these young men and women receive this light. How can they ever be a light to others if they don't receive the light? No pastor can give what he does not have. No pastor can teach what he didn't learn.

> Let your light so shine before men, that they may see your good works, and glorify your Father which is in heaven.
> —MATTHEW 5:16

> The light of the body is the eye: if therefore thine eye be single, thy whole body shall be full of light. But if thine eye be evil, thy whole body shall be full of darkness. If therefore the light that is in thee be darkness, how great is that darkness! No man can serve two masters: for either he will hate the one, and love the other; or else he will hold to the one, and despise the other. Ye cannot serve God and mammon.
> —MATTHEW 6:22–24

Many pastors are graduating from secular schools, struggling to go to seminary at night, and working all day. Many also have wives (or husbands). Some have children and all have a variety of responsibilities. They are instructed by God to love, honor, and provide for these loved ones. If they are to become pastors, they first have to be good husbands and wives, good fathers and mothers. Time becomes too scarce; pastors are forced to choose to do only the bare necessities instead of being afforded the blessings of all that is offered. These young pastors must be provided an environment where they have real prayer time, real study time, as well as time for mentoring from mature, full-grown pastors. This produces pastors who are real trees that can stand the storms that will come and still produce fruit for and from God. This is not just an ideal way; it is not a preferred option. It is the only way we can get fruitful, pastoral trees.

It's our responsibility to take some of their load and insure this needed time. These young trees of God must be able to spend time in the light or they will not grow spiritually. Who wants a tree grown without the full light of Christ? We must wake up! Many of our pastoral trees grown in this unhealthy environment will not produce spiritual fruit. The fruit that has been produced is very evident. Look at the morality of your town, state, and country. True godly trees would have taken a stand, and stood for God, instead of following the whims of people blown about by the winds of popularity. Having experienced several hurricanes and their damage, I see the majority of our pastors today like trees after a major storm. Many were simply blown over because they had no roots at all, while many others were broken in two because they did not have the strength to resist the winds. The overall, vast majority were leaning as the winds blew them. However, thank God, there are always a few who stood straight and tall and refused to bend or break. These are trees which grew in God's light, and received the anointing of God to produce His fruit in abundance.

Part of this devastation is because these trees were mostly grown in seminary schools that are joined to a denominational church. They are being raised with more denominational religious teaching than spiritual teaching. They have more church in them than God. All of those religious people will be offended and may scream, "Not so!" All of the graduated pastors will say not so—that what I'm saying is a lie! If so, I simply would like every one of those with like minds to answer the following question. *Where are the men and women of God, and where and when are they going to take a stand?*

Are they taking a stand now that prayer is no longer allowed in our

55

schools? Are they going to take a stand when the Ten Commandments are to all be burned and cannot be displayed in public? It was okay to take them out of all government buildings. Are they going to stand when there are now ten thousand slaughtered babies a day because five thousand was alright? If homosexuality is an acceptable lifestyle, as is being taught in our schools, will the men and women of God take a stand when it becomes a required course?

Some are taking a verbal stand on gay marriages, and that is good. Why have they not taken a stand on divorce? The divorce rate in the church is now higher than it is in the secular world. If we are going to have preachers preaching, they need to be preaching that divorce is just as much a sin as homosexuality. While they are preaching that, they need to throw in gossip. Here is the real fact: pastors standing in the pulpit that are taking a stand on divorce would be preaching a convicting message to over half of their congregation, very sadly including me. I pray others will be taught what I didn't know and will be equipped to succeed where I failed.

How are we going to get real pastors grown? This will only come about as we each, as individuals, step up and do our part. We cannot wait for the other person or the other church anymore. Growing pastors must start with you and me. We are an important part of what is missing, and it needs to be corrected immediately. We all must individually acknowledge that it is not only the other guys, it is you and me, and we need to step forward to this responsibility first.

Helping our pastors would not be that difficult. We could simply offer to babysit a few hours a week, wash the car, mow the lawn, run errands, take a meal, or even send them out for a nice meal to a good restaurant. Financial support is also almost always lacking. Just think if twenty people "adopted" a young pastor and gave just ten dollars each per week. Can you imagine how it would bless that young chosen vessel of God? Any financial lack in a pastor always shows the spiritual level of the body of Christ. If you are in a church like this and think you can't afford to do any better, you truly do not understand the power of God. Worst of all, you are working from your own capabilities and not God's. This type of mind-set is the result of a lack of God's Word in us. You need to get a good evangelist to come and get some things set right in the body of Christ. When we start to understand and get into a place of faith, so much so that we start working on God's capabilities and not ours, we are going to take back this world. Why shouldn't we? Jesus did!

> Every good gift and every perfect gift is from above, and cometh down from the Father of lights, with whom is no variableness, neither shadow of turning.
>
> —JAMES 1:17

We know God doesn't change and can't lie !

> Even from the days of your fathers ye are gone away from mine ordinances, and have not kept them. Return unto me, and I will return unto you, saith the LORD of hosts. But ye said, Wherein shall we return? Will a man rob God? Yet ye have robbed me. But ye say, Wherein have we robbed thee? In tithes and offerings. Ye are cursed with a curse: for ye have robbed me, even this whole nation. Bring ye all the tithes into the storehouse, that there may be meat in mine house, and prove me now herewith, saith the LORD of hosts, if I will not open you the windows of heaven, and pour you out a blessing, that there shall not be room enough to receive it. And I will rebuke the devourer for your sakes, and he shall not destroy the fruits of your ground; neither shall your vine cast her fruit before the time in the field, saith the LORD of hosts.
>
> —MALACHI 3:7–11

We, as a church, must understand sowing and reaping and how the whole body of Christ is limiting the abilities of God by not understanding this. Claimed Christians who do not tithe, simply believe Satan over God. This costs the whole body of Christ. Godly pastors will quickly lead every one within the body of Christ into the fullness that can come only by tithing.

The national average shows that less than 8 precent of church members tithe. This not only sounds bad, but is bad. It means several things, one being that 92 precent of the people just do not get it. But now get this truth! The faith and obedience of only 8 percent of the people, blessed by God, is capable of carrying the church and the other 92 percent of the unblessed.

Now that is the power of God! When we understand that tithing is more for our benefit than for the church or the pastor, we will start getting Satan out of our lives and getting God in! Here is another real truth: attending a church or acting like a Christian will not benefit you one bit! Christianity simply does not work for the majority of people. Yes, and I will say it again. The truth is that Christianity is not working for the majority of Christians attending church. Why? Because they trust more in the worldly things, which are Satan's, rather than the things of God. Where are our real pastors? God's Word is calling us to righteousness: "That ye put off concerning the former conversation the old man, which is corrupt according to the deceitful lusts; and be renewed in the spirit of your mind; and that ye put on the new man, which after God is created in righteousness and true holiness" (Eph. 4:22–24). There must be evidence of a new man—a real change.

Can't we grow pastors out of most churches? Not when the majority of the congregations want to hear all those "feel-good" messages, that result in no in-depth growth. We hear preachers preach more on prosperity and on how we will be blessed, because the lost don't concern us in a real way. Church congregations do not want to hear or even know about the spiritual warfare that is going on. The church has become all about what God is going to do for them, seldom or never being about what we are to do for God.

Sadly, here is the truth of most of our churches. Many of us have an attitude that God is like a taxi: we whistle, raise a hand, and we are almost immediately picked up and taken where our personal needs are immediately met. This is not you or your church, right? Ask yourselves honestly and recall the prayers of the last four weeks alone. Was the majority of prayer time spent on asking to serve more and praising God, or on something you wanted? Ouch! That hurt a lot of toes, including mine at times. If we really want God and really want to serve God, we must really get serious by clearly understanding that what we have been doing doesn't work. We have been losing, yet we are predestined to be victorious.

Now this is the environment in which the young pastoral trees must grow. In an honest review of our nation and churches, we have a poor environment, in many ways, in which our young pastoral trees can indeed grow. Who is helping them, and what is the real cost for not helping? Can I tell you it may very well be the souls of our children and grandchildren? If only we could understand the cheap cost of raising godly pastors to the enormous costs of not doing so. If we will open our spiritual eyes with a discerning spirit, we will see there are some and maybe many pastors who are of the world more so than of God. These are men and women who started out with the best of intentions, but we failed them at a critical time in their growth. They were grown that way, in that environment, and it now seems normal to us. It is not normal. It is worldly and of Satan!

I would like to know what the total amount of money is that is being spent yearly on drug and alcohol treatment centers. If this county would spend that money on growing pastors, it would change our nation, and we would not need those treatment centers. Now throw in the cost of AIDS treatment and we would literally change the world. Yet, this highly educated country can't see how very happy Satan is with where and how our money is being spent. We can raise money to build prisons and treatment centers, in response to the results of Satan's works. However, this nation and our government will not spend one penny on godly activities.

> For the time will come when they will not endure sound doctrine; but after their own lusts shall they heap to themselves teachers, having itching ears; and they shall turn away their ears from the truth, and shall be turned unto fables.
>
> —2 TIMOTHY 4:3–4

Let me tell you again Satan is very crafty and deceitful at his job. He, who comes to destroy and kill, also has had great success in deceiving. This is where men and women that are called by God are lost to false doctrine, deceived by a bunch of man-made rules that become used by Satan. Then some church becomes led by a group deceived by Satan, not only to burn in hell, but to deceive and lead others straight to hell with them.

Those that are being deceived and doing the deceiving are not at the local fortune teller's, or the sexual fantasy club, nor are they at "Satan-R-Us." They are at the churches and seminary schools. These are the places that resemble godly places, but are not. We, the body of Christ, should be exposing this to the world. We are, in fact, the ones who are promoting this the most. We, in our society, have a driven need for tolerance and have allowed and even accepted and, at times, endorsed un-Christian institutions. We have allowed these not only to exist unopposed, but we have placed them in equality with the Christian-based institutions that stand on the Word of God. This is so prevalent in our culture that tolerance is perceived as a Christian value. A Christian should be the most loving, but the least tolerant, standing firm, but not yielding.

Think for a minute, not with your heart, but with the mind Christ gave you. Why would Satan be down at the sex clubs, and drug users' houses, and other similar places? They are already his, and are only promoting his kingdom. It is you and me that he wants, and he wants to stop what we could really do for God. He wants to stop God's real, fruit-producing churches and pastors. If Satan is not trying to hinder you or your church, you had better look very carefully. Why? He wanted Jesus! He wanted Peter, and I hope he never stops wanting you or me! Thank God for a pastor and God's Word which taught me how to always be victorious over him!

> Be not deceived; God is not mocked: for whatsoever a man soweth, that shall he also reap. For he that soweth to his flesh shall of the flesh reap corruption; but he that soweth to the Spirit shall of the Spirit reap life everlasting.
>
> —GALATIANS 6:7–8

> But evil men and seducers shall wax worse and worse, deceiving, and being deceived. But continue thou in the things which thou hast learned and hast been assured of, knowing of whom thou hast learned them; And that from a child thou hast known the holy scriptures, which are able to make thee wise unto salvation through faith which is in Christ Jesus. All scripture is given by inspiration of God, and is profitable for doctrine, for reproof, for correction, for instruction in righteousness: That

the man of God may be perfect, thoroughly furnished unto all good works.

—2 TIMOTHY 3:13–17

We must understand that many in the church are deceived into thinking they are saved and are doing God's will, but are serving Satan and are lost to an eternal hell. I believe that about half of those who attend church are, in reality, deceived. They are going to be the hardest to reach, and they are doing the greatest for Satan. Just think of how many people you know, or may have even witnessed to, that are not in or want any part of the church because of what a church or self-proclaimed Christian has said and done to them. The burden of these souls should be so profound in us, and to the church, that denominations, differences, and diversities would become completely unimportant to us. We would become unified working together for these precious souls that are so hard to reach. They do not realize they are lost. You and I, who have come to the real truth, God's complete Word, must step up our efforts and reach these precious souls. The best way to reach them is with prayer, love, God's Word, and by His Spirit. It is only the Spirit of God that can reach and touch the very heart of any of us. We need to be in prayer and fasting for these precious souls, inviting the lost, the deceived, the sinners to our churches where the Spirit of God will touch them, heal them, and save them.

Now more than ever, our lives need to be an example to the world of what Jesus really does in us. The world needs to see the real value of a Christian life. Those that are deceived must be able to see Christ in us, the real thing, exposing what is counterfeit.

We must not only be teaching, but equally important, we must be training teachers according to God's Word, and only God's Word. Then we can break Satan's grip and have pastors and teachers of God doing God's work. If not, we will continue to get pastors that are teaching the same false doctrine that deceived them!

First and foremost, we must make sure this is not us. We must be certain that we are standing on God's Word, having studied it for ourselves. Do not allow yourself to just be told by someone else what God's Word says. When is the last time you got out your Bible and really prayed that God would reveal Himself to you through His Word? Have we really accepted His Word as truth? Does He really mean what His Word says? God has given us a lot of scriptures on knowledge and wisdom. He expects us to know His Word if we know His Son. In fact, I question how we can know Jesus without knowing God's Word? There are many who, after accepting the wonderful mercy and grace of God, never read God's Word, never attend any Bible study, and seldom attend church! They have, however, over time developed a whole religion in their minds and how spiritual matters should be. The hard truth is that to some extent this is all of us. When we start to understand this, we will understand Jesus is the *Word!* Here are some examples of what God has to say about knowledge and wisdom:

> That in every thing ye are enriched by him, in all utterance, and in all knowledge; Even as the testimony of Christ was confirmed in you: So that ye come behind in no gift; waiting for the coming of our Lord Jesus Christ: Who shall also confirm you unto the end, that ye may be blameless in the day of our Lord Jesus Christ. God is faithful, by whom ye were called unto the fellowship of his Son Jesus Christ our Lord.
>
> —1 CORINTHIANS 1:5–9

> For to one is given by the Spirit the word of wisdom; to another the word of knowledge by the same Spirit.
>
> —1 CORINTHIANS 12:8

> For God, who commanded the light to shine out of darkness, hath shined in our hearts, to give the light of the knowledge of the glory of God in the face of Jesus Christ. But we have this treasure in earthen vessels, that the excellency of the power may be of God, and not of us.
>
> —2 CORINTHIANS 4:6–7

> That the God of our Lord Jesus Christ, the Father of glory, may give unto you the spirit of wisdom and revelation in the knowledge of him: the eyes of your understanding being enlightened; that ye may know what is the hope of his calling, and what the riches of the glory of his inheritance in the saints, and what is the

exceeding greatness of his power to us-ward who believe, according to the working of his mighty power, which he wrought in Christ, when he raised him from the dead, and set him at his own right hand in the heavenly places, far above all principality, and power, and might, and dominion, and every name that is named, not only in this world, but also in that which is to come: And hath put all things under his feet, and gave him to be the head over all things to the church, Which is his body, the fulness of him that filleth all in all.

—EPHESIANS 1:17–23

And this I pray, that your love may abound yet more and more in knowledge and in all judgment; That ye may approve things that are excellent; that ye may be sincere and without offence till the day of Christ. Being filled with the fruits of righteousness, which are by Jesus Christ, unto the glory and praise of God.

—PHILIPPIANS 1:9–11

Who is a wise man and endued with knowledge among you? let him shew out of a good conversation his works with meekness of wisdom. But if ye have bitter envying and strife in your hearts, glory not, and lie not against the truth. This wisdom descendeth not from above, but is earthly, sensual, devilish. For where envying and strife is, there is confusion and every evil work. But the wisdom that is from above is first pure, then peaceable, gentle, and easy to be intreated, full of mercy and good fruits, without partiality, and without hypocrisy. And the fruit of righteousness is sown in peace of them that make peace.

—JAMES 3:13–18

But grow in grace, and in the knowledge of our Lord and Saviour Jesus Christ. To him be glory both now and for ever. Amen.

—2 PETER 3:18

We must get our Bibles out, get on our knees, and get it right. No one is going to go to hell for us or in our place. There is no return warranty program, no thirty-day trials; we will be judged according to our decisions and choices. It's up to us. It may seem unfair, but your eternal life will be about your own choices. Wrong choices made with right motives or false knowledge and understanding will be just the same as bad choices. Satan will be laughing at our stupid defense, for there is no excuse. God gave us His Word. God then manifested His Word in Jesus. God gave us His gifts: the gift of His very Spirit. He loved us so much He gave us His very best. What we have given Him in return will be judged. We can start with giving to His pastors all that is required so they can grow His kingdom God's way and not man's.

In love and concern let me be very clear. It is important and hard when I write about denominational churches, activities and programs, and about helping real pastors to be God's pastors and only God's pastors. When I mention about how it can no longer be man's way, if you're starting to get puffed up, angry, and insulted, you're probably one of those being deceived. Satan has you fooled, your mind first, next your emotions, and then your actions. We all must become wise and learn to trust in only God's Word, not some man-made agreement, and not your thoughts and feelings! The last thing Satan would want is for you to see the truth. Satan always presents the truth as a lie. We all must learn to understand how Satan works on us to prevent us from being the overcomers God established us to be. Sometimes the truth hurts. For your own spiritual life, forever and forever, please get these truths. This is not only for your life, but for the lives of your children and all those you could reach.

Imagine that as you burn in hell you hear your kids scream, "Why did you feed me these lies? Mommy, Daddy, why didn't you tell me the truth?" Your good intentions or what you thought was right will not make a difference. No church membership book will save you, an excuse of "I was told wrong" or "It's not my fault" will not be acceptable either. There is no substitute for knowing the Word of God. I think this scene is going to be real, played over and over, because Satan has deceived generation after generation, and all will literally burn in hell. If we do not know the truth, how will we know a lie? I pray that if absolutely nothing I have written is understood but this sentence, this sentence will be remembered: we must know the difference between a lie and the truth. Without this understanding, we may well be pruning God off, and leaving Satan to grow. Pray, pray, and then get serious and pray.

> For every one that doeth evil hateth the light, neither cometh to the light, lest his deeds should be reproved. But he that doeth truth cometh to the light, that his deeds may be made manifest, that they are wrought in God.
>
> —JOHN 3:20–21

Please read and take to heart these words, they are expressed in love, with a great burden for the lost. Over and over in the Scriptures, God is calling, instructing, and correcting us by His Word. We must understand that before the foundations of the earth, God knew us. God knew us and chose us while we were still sinners, loved us while we loved the things of this world. The Bible is the inspired Word of God and was written just as much for us in this day as it was for those living thousands of years ago. I was taught to put my name in places in the Bible where it shows someone else's name. It was written to me and for me because God knew me, just as God knows you.

> I charge thee [RON] therefore before God, and the Lord Jesus Christ, who shall judge the quick and the dead at his appearing and his kingdom; Preach the word; be instant in season, out of season; reprove, rebuke, exhort with all long suffering and doctrine. For the time will come when they will not endure sound doctrine; but after their own lusts shall they heap to themselves teachers, having itching ears; And they shall turn away their ears from the truth, and shall be turned unto fables. But watch thou in all things, endure afflictions, do the work of an evangelist, make full proof of thy ministry.
>
> —2 TIMOTHY 4:1–5

> And because ye [RON] are sons, God hath sent forth the Spirit of his Son into your hearts, crying, Abba, Father. Wherefore thou art no more a servant, but a son; and if a son, then an heir of God through Christ.
>
> —GALATIANS 4:6–7

> That your [RON'S] faith should not stand in the wisdom of men, but in the power of God. Howbeit we speak wisdom among them that are perfect: yet not the wisdom of this world, nor of the

princes of this world, that come to nought: But we speak the wisdom of God in a mystery, even the hidden wisdom, which God ordained before the world unto our glory:

—1 Corinthians 2:5–7

This Word is alive and will always be alive. The power of the Word of God is unlimited, as well as the understanding and knowledge it gives. We all have every bit of information that is needed for our whole lives.

The Word will tell us how to be a child; it will tell us how to be an adult. It will tell us how to be a husband or wife. It will tell us how to be a father or mother. It gives us instructions for every part of our lives. It tells us how to prosper and how to rise above disappointments and disasters. We learn how to live and how to die. When followed, we learn how to have peace and joy in this life, and riches in the life to come. It's clearly a living gospel, which is about choices that can only be made with the true knowledge of God's Word.

I call heaven and earth to record this day against you, that I have set before you life and death, blessing and cursing: therefore choose life, that both thou and thy seed may live.

—Deuteronomy 30:19

I hope we all can see the importance of getting a pastor into the light of God, grown on His Word and undefiled by man. We have lost generations to the ignorance and pride we all must overcome. It's too important! We have lost and are losing too many.

When Ron Gordon says that every other Christian is going to hell, it means absolutely nothing. Many people that just read this have completely discounted it, thinking it is ridiculous and can't even begin to be accurate. That Gordon fellow got off the elevator way before it reached the top floor. Maybe so, but how about someone who went past the top floor, and ascended all the way to heaven, to be at the right hand of the Father? How about Jesus? How many did He say would be lost? Remember, Jesus is Lord and Savior, but He is also the greatest prophet to walk the earth. Every Word Jesus spoke has come true, except one. He has not yet returned. Thank God He has not. There is still time. Now let us look at Jesus' words.

Then shall the kingdom of heaven be likened unto ten virgins, which took their lamps, and went forth to meet the bridegroom. And five of them were wise, and five were foolish. They that were foolish took their lamps, and took no oil with them: But the wise took oil in their vessels with their lamps. While the bridegroom tarried, they all slumbered and slept. And at midnight there was a cry made, Behold, the bridegroom cometh; go ye out to meet him. Then all those virgins arose, and trimmed their lamps. And the foolish said unto the wise, Give us of your oil; for our lamps are gone out. But the wise answered, saying, Not so; lest there be not enough for us and you: but go ye rather to them that sell, and buy for yourselves. And while they went to buy, the bridegroom came; and they that were ready went in with him to the marriage: and the door was shut. Afterward came also the other virgins, saying, Lord, Lord, open to us. But he answered and said, Verily I say unto you, I know you not.

—MATTHEW 25:1–12

The door was shut and half were left out. Five wise and five foolish— or fifty percent.

Then shall two be in the field; the one shall be taken, and the other left.

—MATTHEW 24:40

Two in the field: one is taken and one is left—or fifty percent.

Two women shall be grinding at the mill; the one shall be taken, and the other left.

—MATTHEW 24:41

Two at the mill: one is taken and one is left again– or fifty percent.

Now it is important for us to understand these scriptures. The first thing people think is, "Well, they were worldly and not involved in a church." Look again, Jesus is the bridegroom and we are the bride who awaits His return. That is us, the church, and it is the bride of Christ that the door was shut on. Furthermore, it is Christ who shuts the door. If we are to prevent many of the deceived from going to hell, we must start in the church. We must come to understand that for the most part, the heathen that are lost know they are lost. Not all, but most just think they will have time for God later. I heard a joke once that I have always remembered. I believe it is so true:

> Satan sent his demons from hell to the people on earth and told them to tell the people that there is no God. The demons returned to hell. Satan asked, "How did it work?" They answered, "Not well. There is something in the human spirit that they just know there is really a God." Satan sent them back and said, "Tell them there is no devil or hell." Again, upon their return, they reported that there is just something in human spirit that they know there is a devil and a hell. Satan thought for some time and then sent them all back and told them, "Just tell the people they have plenty of time." Upon their return they were ecstatic. "It worked," they said, "the people believe that they have plenty of time!"

Most of us have been there. Thank God, Jesus didn't return before we were ready. But we, you and I, must save the others!

It is the lost in the church who don't even know they are lost, and won't begin to believe Satan has deceived them. They will be the hardest to reach. They are also the ones who make it difficult to change the church. Satan will puff up their pride, making it more difficult and harder. We must be able to reach them to help them, as well as others. They can be identified the same as we can, by the fruit they are producing, or the lack of. We all need to start with a self-examination. Are we producing fruit? What is the fruit that we, as individuals, have produced? This must not start with what our church is doing, but with what we are doing. When we stand before the great judgment seat we will not stand with our church. We will be judged alone. What our particular church, denomination, or any other affiliation did or did not accomplish will not be a part of our judgment.

I believe we that know the truth, being well able to discern right from wrong according to God's Word, cannot continue to stand idly by. We must be about reaching the lost and restoring them and the church. It is just going to take some of us to say, "I will," and then do what God has for us to accomplish.

I have so much to learn, so far to go. However, this I do know: there are no accidents in God or His people! You and I were birthed for this time and this work. I did not write this book by accident, and you didn't purchase it by accident. The only question is whether we live up to our calling and birthright.

> And many false prophets shall rise, and shall deceive many. And because iniquity shall abound, the love of many shall wax cold. But he that shall endure unto the end, the same shall be saved.
> —MATTHEW 24:11–13

I have tried to explain how pastors must be raised by God and not by man. When we fix ourselves, we will be fixing the church. I have tried to point to the facts that show we are failing as a church, as a body that should be the bride of Christ. I, in no way, ever want to make the wonderful gift of mercy and grace less than what it is—which is a great gift from God! Do we, however, really believe that what we have been offering to God and what we have become is an acceptable bride for Jesus, the King of kings and Lord of lords? It should be that each and every one of us would be worthy to walk down the aisle to our groom, but are we? I believe that we are to become worthy, however, not by our own accomplishment, but by Jesus' accomplishments.

Pastors, leaders, and every individual in a church should consider this: what would you say, how would you feel, if on this day you were to introduce the Christ, the Son of God, to His bride, your church? My Lord, my King, my God, "Well done, good and faithful servant." Would we be embarrassed knowing we are presenting an unworthy bride? I believe this is going to be a real event in our lives. Few will find this a wondrous day, a day of great excitement and joy as weddings should be.

It is imperative that we know how important this is and why. Please, people of the church, brothers and sisters, give this prayerful attention. We must understand this. We do not have to be a graduate of some seminary, our intelligence does not have to be real great to figure this one out. All we have to do is listen to God and read His Word to get this.

Where are the false prophets going to be? Where will they be the most

69

effective? They are not only in and representing many churches; in many cases they are the church. They are speaking in our churches, teaching in our churches, but what they are speaking and teaching is not the gospel of Jesus, the Christ. It is very close. It sometimes sounds real, but it is a counterfeit, and can be found to be such by its fruit. We must always be searching and examining the fruit as well as what and who is sowing. Start right now and make sure every word spoken in your Sunday schools and by those who teach any class are of God. If you're well grounded in the Word, sit in on every class and see what is being taught. Correct anything that is wrong. If it's not exactly the Word of God, it is wrong. Every teacher who seeks after God will be pleased to have any errors pointed out. Those who don't should not be teaching in the first place. Check every word from the pulpit, especially with our young and growing pastors.

Hold every pastor's feet to the Word of God. Pastors can and will make mistakes. When the mistakes are scriptural, they need to be pointed out. Again, any pastor that is truly called by God will always thank you for pointing out any errors. If the pastor is told in love and humility, and he rises up in pride, or argumentatively objects, prune deep and expose him to large amounts of God's light. A prideful pastor is doing Satan's work, not God's. His fruit will be fruit unto man, not God.

Please be extremely respectful of our pastors, and their time. Do not correct them in front of anyone just to show how great you are. Also make sure you're right first, you will not be any help if the pastor has to show you where you are incorrect all the time. This is real, godly stuff for real Christians, the servants! We are to be building and growing a pastor, and that will always be about lifting up God's chosen. Raising, growing, encouraging, equipping, and providing financially—that is how we grow pastor!

There are many godly, mature pastors who are experienced and filled with knowledge. These pastors can and should be used in the growing process. They not only can guide these young pastors, but can lend guidance to all of us. Many have studied the Word of God well, and carry an anointing to teach and preach. There are many schools and churches striving to be in God's will. They must be supported as well as used. They again can be determined by their fruit and how they stand for the Word of God. Pastors after God's heart are needed badly, and needed now. We have allowed compromise, instead of standing for righteousness. We have settled for tranquility and lost the peace of God. Hell is real, and many are there because you and I failed them and failed our Lord. We all must understand that only those who endure unto the end will be saved. So many souls are lost and going to hell because we, as a church, have allowed Satan to have his way. We all are too proud to think it's not me, my family, or my church. This must be about some other church. I hear it all the time—my church this and my church that. There is only one book, and our name is only placed there by the blood of Jesus. There is no other way to escape the lake of fire, people need to hear the truth about hell.

We hear some say, "I just don't believe God would allow Satan in our church." We need to be telling them that he didn't! We are opening the doors wider to his ways ever day. Now we all, and I mean *all*, must really ask ourselves this question: if half of the church is lost, is it even possible I am one of the lost? If God is warning us that there will be ministers of Satan in our churches, is it our minister? It must be some of us, and it must be some of our ministers. Examine yourself by God's Word, not by any other book or means. Inspect the fruit. There must be fruit and it must be godly!

Satan is the prince of this world. Please understand his power and position. Many times he is manifested in the people who believe they have led a good life, and therefore will not go to hell. Church, can we even begin to count those that are lost and burning because of this demon alone? Yes, it is a demon, a demon of deception. If you don't believe it, he may already have you deceived. The fact is, many of these people are basically good and probably better than most. The real facts and truths are that when Jesus judges, it will not be based on the curve, the supreme court, or a majority vote. It will be based on the everlasting Word of God, and every word that has proceeded out of Jesus' mouth. Only the blood of Jesus will save any of us, and we must be in a relationship with Him to have the blood wash our sinful lives clean.

Here is another one of those keys! Having had a brief conversation one day with or about Jesus is not a relationship. Our relationship is as a bride, it is to be intimate and consummated. It takes more than just saying, "I do," to be married.

We have come to a conclusion that since our nation and its laws have changed, our morality seems normal. We think that God has changed and our behavior is acceptable to Him. God cannot change. His Word says so. In Malachi 3:6, it states: "For I am the Lord, I change not; therefore ye sons of Jacob are not consumed." But we just continue getting closer to hell, gaining speed, and calling it freedom. The closer we get, the faster we travel in hell's direction and the more Satan influences our lives. As he did with Eve, we have become convinced we are right, not by God's words, but by man's.

> Jesus answered and said unto him, If a man love me, he will keep my words: and my Father will love him, and we will come unto him, and make our abode with him. He that loveth me not keepeth not my sayings: and the word which ye hear is not mine, but the Father's which sent me. These things have I spoken unto you, being yet present with you. But the Comforter, which is the Holy Ghost, whom the Father will send in my name, he shall teach you all things, and bring all things to your remembrance, whatsoever I have said unto you. Peace I leave with you, my peace I give unto you: not as the world giveth, give I unto you. Let not your heart be troubled, neither let it be afraid. Ye have heard how I said unto you, I go away, and come again unto you. If ye loved me, ye would rejoice, because I said, I go unto the Father: for my Father is greater than I. And now I have told you before it come to pass, that, when it is come to pass, ye might believe. Hereafter I will not talk much with you: for the prince of this world cometh, and hath nothing in me. But that the world may know that I love the Father; and as the Father gave me commandment, even so I do. Arise, let us go hence.
>
> —JOHN 14:23–31

He that loves and keeps His words will abide with Jesus and the Father. Again, the Word of God will last forever. If we do not know this Word for ourselves, instead of what someone has said it means, how do we know what is truth? Satan is a liar and the father of it.

After all of God's warnings and teachings, how can we keep falling for the same old lies? If we have not allowed the Holy Ghost to read the Word of God with us, giving us the real truth, we cannot know the truth. We must read the Word and be open prayerfully to letting God speak to us, guide us, correct us, and be in charge of our lives. When we read the Word of God, we must start with prayer, asking God that by His Spirit He will give us truth, knowledge, and understanding, His Word says He will. God's Word is true, even though we do not always understand all of it's meanings all at once. Christianity, along with understanding, is a process, not an overnight miracle. Moses spent forty days on Mount Sinai and still had difficulties. Growth in Christ will only come by spending time in God's Word. God's Word is alive: it is real.

Either Jesus is the Christ, the Word manifested in the flesh and by His blood, and we are cleansed to be acceptable to a living God, or our great, great, great, great grandpa was an ape. The fact is either Darwin is right, or all of the prophets are right. Many are resigned to wait until death to know, not coming to the understanding that we serve a living God. He is still doing, answering prayers, saving the lost, and destroying the works of Satan. My God is still the God that healeth thee!

> Verily, verily, I say unto you, If a man keep my saying, he shall never see death.
> —JOHN 8:51

> For there shall arise false Christs, and false prophets, and shall shew great signs and wonders; insomuch that, if it were possible, they shall deceive the very elect. Behold, I have told you before.
> —MATTHEW 24:24–25

> For they that are such serve not our Lord Jesus Christ, but their own belly; and by good words and fair speeches deceive the hearts of the simple. For your obedience is come abroad unto all men. I am glad therefore on your behalf: but yet I would have you wise unto that which is good, and simple concerning evil.
> —ROMANS 16:18–19

Read God's Word, read God's Word, read God's Word, and look at what these scriptures say. Jesus told us, "Hereafter I will not talk much with you: *for the prince of this world cometh*, and hath nothing in me" (John 14:30, emphasis added). Satan is the prince of this world, and we need to be teaching our brothers and sisters how to overcome his power and influence. How can we teach them if they don't even know he is their real enemy? Satan tries to steal their salvation, their blessings, and the gifts that God has for them. God's Word says that He comes immediately. Consider the parable of the sower. "And these are they by the way side, where the word is sown; but when they have heard, Satan cometh immediately, and taketh away the word that was sown in their hearts" (Mark 4:15). Where are the pastors who are preaching the knowledge of Satan's presence and power? Satan is as real as salvation, and we must have knowledge to defeat him.

Many congregations just want to be given another "feel-good" sermon and then be left alone. We must grow pastors who preach what is needed and not what is wanted! How many parents do you know that gave their children what they wanted instead of what they really needed. These parents encouraged unhealthy wants in love, through ignorance. Where are these children now? The vast majority are in prisons, drug rehabs, mental institutions, and dysfunctional families everywhere. We, as a nation, need spiritual fathers who will give us what is needed, not what we want.

Our churches have let Satan steal the salvation of generations that are too proud and self-centered to return to God's Word. We now must be growing pastors to reach the church, before the church can reach the world. I hope you can see the truth here. The church needs to save the world and we must be saving the church

> For every one that useth milk is unskilful in the word of righteousness: for he is a babe. But strong meat belongeth to them that are of full age, even those who by reason of use have their senses exercised to discern both good and evil.
>
> —HEBREWS 5:13–14

> Now is the judgment of this world: now shall the prince of this world be cast out. And I, if I be lifted up from the earth, will draw all men unto me.
>
> —JOHN 12:31–32

> Wherein in time past ye walked according to the course of this world, according to the prince of the power of the air, the spirit that now worketh in the children of disobedience: Among whom also we all had our conversation in times past in the lusts of our flesh, fulfilling the desires of the flesh and of the mind; and were by nature the children of wrath, even as others. —EPHESIANS 2:2–3

Now that our young pastor is going to begin to bud out in blossoms, we must be sure he blossoms with God's fruit. I hope we can now see that everything of man must be pruned. Man is sinful in nature, and in our best intentions, we will get it wrong. Prune off your particular church doctrine. We all must understand that as these pastors grow fruit, it will either be fruit of doctrine, or the fruit of God. God or man, it is that simple. Whose fruit do you want? We must prune off the outside influences when growing a pastor. A pastor submitting to this board or that committee to keep his job is going to take that congregation straight to hell. Board members who want to control the pastor are doing the work of Satan. If you are on a board or committee, please understand what your scriptural duties really are.

You are a servant, not a boss, probably more anointed to see that the toilet is clean, than to give scriptural advice to one of God's chosen vessels. Elders and deacons have a place and God's authority to do great and needful works. It's important we know what these works are.

> Wherefore, brethren, look ye out among you seven men of honest report, full of the Holy Ghost and wisdom, whom we may appoint over this business. But we will give ourselves continually to prayer, and to the ministry of the word.
>
> —ACTS 6:3–4

The first men appointed were to allow the apostles to give themselves to prayer and the ministry of the Word. In a church that is operating correctly, the elders and deacons take on providing many of the needs of the body of Christ. We must teach all members of our churches to have faith and confidence in our elders and deacons. They need to understand that these men of God can and should be praying for them, having the same results as any pastor. It's not the elders, it's not the deacons, and it's not the pastors, it is Jesus in them. Answered prayers are not because of one's title—as an elder, a deacon, or a pastor—but rather they are from the Spirit of God in them, as well as in you and me.

The same Jesus is in all of them, as well as in you and me. Every elder and deacon should be comfortable going to homes and hospitals to pray for the sick. If not, they are not an elder or deacon fulfilling God's plan. These mighty men of God can and should help the pastor in so many ways. Their positions are worthy to obtain. In larger churches, the church could not operate without them. We all must understand their authority. God appoints a pastor, a pastor appoints an elder or deacon. If this is done correctly, elders and deacons are in authority over us, and we are to be in submission to them. I personally have no respect for an elder or deacon in office simply because of a majority vote. Many of these "elected" do not even meet the qualifications, and they are nothing more than men appointed to some board resembling a political office. There is no anointing on their lives, and they can only walk or work in the natural, not in the spiritual. Try to find this procedure in God's Word. Many churches fail in not understanding that the anointing of God will only, and I mean only, flow through God's appointed authority.

This book is not about elders and deacons, so I will not spend a lot of time here. I do, however, want two things clearly understood. First, elders and deacons are not to be in authority over a pastor that has been called by God. Those of you that are power-hungry control freaks, get your hands off our pastors. Secondly, real elders and deacons are mighty warriors in the kingdom of God. They are to be in authority over us, the congregation. They are there for us. They are to help and guide us. Pray for them. They are God's chosen and anointed vessels. These elders and deacons will be a major part in the last great revival. Support them!

> And when they had ordained them elders in every church, and had prayed with fasting, they commended them to the Lord, on whom they believed.
>
> —ACTS 14:23

Elders and deacons, know this please: the more anointed your pastor is and the more works your church is doing for God, the more Satan wants your pastor and you. Satan will always go for the head first. Your first priority is to protect your pastor. We have seen great ministries fall because of sin in a man of God. Protect your pastor, get in front of him or her. Do not allow Satan to have your leader. Jesus prayed for Peter and the others. Should you do less? Jesus said Satan wanted Peter to sift him as wheat. Satan wants your pastor if he or she is doing God's work. The temptations will be continual and will vary. Most of the time, temptations will be aimed at the lusts of man. Sex, money, pride, and power can be powerful temptations and many will fall without help. Beware and be prepared to battle. Go to war for your pastor.

If you and your church have not fasted and prayed over your elders and deacons, set a date and do it. Do it often and fast for them. They not only deserve your prayers, they need them. Have a day of fasting and bring them before God and the congregation in prayer with the laying on of hands and anointing them with oil. Elders and deacons can and should be a powerful godly force in our churches. This force has not been used to its fullest capacity. We need it badly in our churches. It will require mighty elders and deacons to raise mighty pastors.

> Let the elders that rule well be counted worthy of double honour, especially they who labor in the word and doctrine.
>
> —1 TIMOTHY 5:17

> Is any sick among you? let him call for the elders of the church; and let them pray over him, anointing him with oil in the name of the Lord.
>
> —JAMES 5:14

A lot has been said on this topic, but it needed to be said. Great churches—great not in number or size, but great in the Word and works of God—will have a pastor in full liberty to God, and only God. I know many great, mighty elders called by God that can pray over you to be healed, yet clean the restrooms the same day. They will thank God that He considered them worthy to do either, and they know it is Jesus in them. They will give their best to the toilets, the pastor, the congregation, and stay prepared to do battle on a moment's notice. These are God's elders and deacons. Now put these men in your pastor's workforce correctly and you are going to see God's will being done. Churches will start taking back what Satan has stolen.

Also, prune your pastor, especially young, blooming pastors, of work that can be done by others. Do you want a pastor full of faith? I mean when someone is told that they have cancer, theses pastors are vessels who know that by the authority given them by God, they can pray for every disease and sickness and the people will be healed. Pastors need to be grown only to know victory in Christ. That kind of faith "cometh by hearing, and hearing by the word of God" (Rom. 10:17).

This is the time that a young pastor has to be allowed time to be in the Word of God. There is no other choice. A young pastor needs to be in prayer and study, and I mean hours and hours, and more hours. It's harder for smaller churches where the pastor has to both pray and paint. True growth for the pastor and church will start when others start doing the maintenance. We sometimes confuse the scripture:

> For as the body without the spirit is dead, so faith without works is dead also.
>
> —JAMES 2:26

Decide what kind of works you want your pastor to do. How much time does your pastor spend on cleaning, maintenance, programs, errands, and other miscellaneous stuff that volunteers could be doing? No pastor will be able to give you godly faith with scripturally sound teaching if they do not have it to give. This takes time in God's Word and presence.

> Remember them which have the rule over you, who have spoken
> unto you the word of God: whose faith follow, considering the
> end of their conversation.
>
> —HEBREWS 13:7

Those that have rule over you "have spoken unto you the word of
God." This is our pastors, elders, and deacons. They are warriors prepared to do battle, armed with the sword of the Spirit.

> And Jesus said unto them, Because of your unbelief: for verily I
> say unto you, If ye have faith as a grain of mustard seed, ye shall
> say unto this mountain, Remove hence to yonder place; and it
> shall remove; and nothing shall be impossible unto you.
>
> —MATTHEW 17:20

More than likely, we all are going to need help, spiritual help, scriptural healing, prayer for our lost children, and healing when our hearts
are broken. We will need a pastor that is full of faith and not just a
person who sounds great praying. When Satan has had his way, and
we are in need of help, do we want someone who has been in study,
prayer, and fasting or someone who just mowed the church lawn! Get
real here! You may be the one needing prayer. There is a difference
in demons, there is a difference in how we are prepared. When the
demonic spirit of death comes to you or your family, who is going to
be capable of defeating it and sending it back to hell?

> Howbeit this kind goeth not out but by prayer and fasting.
>
> —MATTHEW 17:21

In recapping, it is not too hard to prune a young budding pastor.
Simply know the Word of God, and prune off anything man-made.
Prune off everything possible that takes their time from prayer and
studying. Most of all make sure there is nothing of Satan in us that
needs to be pruned. Your pastor will be attacked by Satan and must
have the tools to be capable of fighting off these attacks. These tools
are the Word of God in them and our prayers. The power of a praying
church is mighty. Pray for your pastor.

Peter therefore was kept in prison: but prayer was made without ceasing of the church unto God for him. And when Herod would have brought him forth, the same night Peter was sleeping between two soldiers, bound with two chains: and the keepers before the door kept the prison. And, behold, the angel of the Lord came upon him, and a light shined in the prison: and he smote Peter on the side, and raised him up, saying, Arise up quickly. And his chains fell off from his hands.

—ACTS 12:5–7

Jesus is the same yesterday, today, and forever. Pray for your pastor and pray for your church to be God's church. Pray in unity and in numbers. Now that we know we must be growing and learning to raise a pastor, we must also be more than able to pray for ourselves. Pray that, by the Spirit of the living God, we will not be a hindrance or a problem, and that we will not allow ourselves to be used by Satan.

We all need to regularly be in the sanctuary of God, on our knees and faces, praying for forgiveness and discernment, constantly applying the blood of Christ to our lives. Only after this self-judging and cleansing are we able to prune.

Chapter Four

TREES OF GREATNESS

T he seedling pastors have now grown, or we have a transplanted one which is beginning to produce fruit. These pastors still need tending to, perhaps more so than ever before. Every tree that is producing, or going to produce, a lot of fruit will need a lot of care. Great producers will need great care. Small producers will need much less care. Talk to the pastors of great ministries and they will tell you straight up that what makes the difference is, first and foremost, Jesus, followed by their staff, associates, and congregation. Many congregations desire to have a great pastor and ministry like they read about or see on television. They do not, however, want to put forth the effort or pay the price. If they could just pray it into existence they would. We, as the body of Christ, need to understand it takes great effort and sacrifice along with prayer to grow great pastors and ministries. It is time that these ministries that are doing great works, being in the center of God's will, speak out the truth as to how they were grown and the cost.

To grow these pastors and ministries we must start with the right pastoral tree. These trees must undergo, and be able to pass, inspection. These inspections are very important and must be done early on in the tree's growth to find the flaws and defects that must be removed.

We must start the inspection of the pastoral tree itself. What is its character, personality, and appearance? What is its very moral fiber or being? As always, the correct starting point is important when inspecting anything, especially a pastor. Have we learned to always start in the Word of God?

> For with what judgment ye judge, ye shall be judged: and with what measure ye mete, it shall be measured to you again. And why beholdest thou the mote that is in thy brother's eye, but considerest not the beam that is in thine own eye? Or how wilt thou say to thy brother, Let me pull out the mote out of thine eye; and, behold, a beam is in thine own eye? Thou hypocrite, first cast out the beam out of thine own eye; and then shalt thou see clearly to cast out the mote out of thy brother's eye.
>
> —MATTHEW 7:2–5

If we have taken to heart the previous chapters, then you're well on your way in the self-examination process. There should be an internal fire started where we have begun to burn away the chaff and all the worldly stuff out of ourselves. It will have become self-evident that we must keep that fire burning at all times. We must know, first and foremost, that we need a fire of constant self-cleansing and purging. Then, and only then, can we become a pastoral tree and fruit inspector. This is by far the hardest part of growing a pastor. Preparing ourselves is a hard and often painful undertaking. It is the hardest part for a pastor also.

Good pastors spend their entire lives in the purging and cleansing fire of God. Not only must a pastor go through all that we do, and even more so, but during the process, he must be growing us as well. The needs of the flock are many and sometimes draining for every pastor. When we work on the "us," the part that is really hard is always "I." This self-work must be done first, then we can enhance the pastoral growing process immensely.

We are now inspecting a maturing or grown tree that has produced fruit. We must always remember that every pastor is called by God and has, hopefully, been prayerfully placed by God and is doing the works of God. The fruit will always be the guiding factor. As we inspect, we must be assured it's godly. If it's not godly fruit; it's not a godly pastor.

We spent a lot of time on this in the last chapter, but again, not all pastors are godly, or even of or about God. Sometimes they might be the most loveable and enjoyable people we have ever met. Great! Please understand that does not make them a godly pastor. We have to recognize that not all pastors are godly, as well as all churches are not of God. It's our responsibility to know the difference, and the Word of God will always guide us, instruct us, and should always be the standard we use to measure, inspect, and judge. Judge the fruit not the person! Jesus taught us very clearly to always look at the fruit.

> A good tree cannot bring forth evil fruit, neither can a corrupt tree bring forth good fruit. Every tree that bringeth not forth good fruit is hewn down, and cast into the fire. Wherefore by their fruits ye shall know them.
> —MATTHEW 7:18–20

> For every tree is known by his own fruit. For of thorns men do not gather figs, nor of a bramble bush gather they grapes. A good man out of the good treasure of his heart bringeth forth that which is good; and an evil man out of the evil treasure of his heart bringeth forth that which is evil: for of the abundance of the heart his mouth speaketh. And why call ye me, Lord, Lord, and do not the things which I say?
> —LUKE 6:44–46

This is the most critical part of any Christians' walk. Everyone must first understand that we, and only we as individuals, are responsible to see that we are in fact serving, worshiping, and believing in the one true and living God. As I pointed out earlier, many without knowing it are deceived into a religion or church doctrine that looks and acts like a church, but is not.

> Take heed to yourselves, that your heart be not deceived, and ye turn aside, and serve other gods, and worship them.
> —DEUTERONOMY 11:16

> Let not him that is deceived trust in vanity: for vanity shall be his recompence. It shall be accomplished before his time, and his

branch shall not be green. He shall shake off his unripe grape as the vine, and shall cast off his flower as the olive. For the congregation of hypocrites shall be desolate, and fire shall consume the tabernacles of bribery. They conceive mischief, and bring forth vanity, and their belly prepareth deceit.

—JOB 15:31–35

Be not deceived: evil communications corrupt good manners. Awake to righteousness, and sin not; for some have not the knowledge of God: I speak this to your shame.

—1 CORINTHIANS 15:33–34

For we ourselves also were sometimes foolish, disobedient, deceived, serving divers lusts and pleasures, living in malice and envy, hateful, and hating one another. But after that the kindness and love of God our Saviour toward man appeared.

—TITUS 3:3–4

We must therefore become a qualified fruit inspector, having the knowledge and understanding of the Word of God. We will also have to know who we are in Christ. Self-judging our real intentions and our hearts is crucial! Above and before all things we must have this right.

Grace be with all them that love our Lord Jesus Christ in sincerity. Amen.

—EPHESIANS 6:24

To whom God would make known what is the riches of the glory of this mystery among the Gentiles; which is Christ in you, the hope of glory: Whom we preach, warning every man, and teaching every man in all wisdom; that we may present every man perfect in Christ Jesus: Whereunto I also labour, striving according to his working, which worketh in me mightily.

—COLOSSIANS 1:27–29

This is only possible by Christ in us. We are to be Christlike, and here is always a good inspection area. For example, when people see us, do they see Christ in us? If not, we are failing. When we look at our pastors and church leaders, do we see Christ in them? If the answer to these questions is no, then there is a problem, and we need to fix it, and fix it quickly. If anyone professes to be a Christian and does not set forth the examples of Christ, then they must be setting forth the examples of Satan. There is no middle ground, no neutral corner, we are either serving Jesus or Satan.

There are two major questions which measure the extent and purpose of our lives: first, are we serving? Second, whom are we serving? This is as real a hell, as important as salvation, and we the church body must get it right. We have not arrived yet, but if we had pastors of the Jehovah God, we could!

> Neither be ye called masters: for one is your Master, even Christ.
> But he that is greatest among you shall be your servant.
> —MATTHEW 23:10–11

We are to be servants, with the full understanding that servants are to serve. Servanthood is always our first and continual calling. If we are not one of the best servants in our church, helping in all needful areas and not just where we want to be, we are not ready to be a pastoral tree or fruit inspector. By the time a pastor is producing fruit, working to save souls, and spiritually feeding the flock, the very last thing they would need is an unqualified fruit nitpicker. If we are not serving our church in a real and meaningful way, but think we should have some authority, without any doubt we are a nitpicker. No matter the well-meant intentions, a nitpicker is going against God's will. We must grow up, get on our knees, repent, pray, seek, and start serving the needs of our church body. Otherwise, we need to get out of the way of those who truly seek to serve their Lord. If we spend a lot of time explaining to people how things should be done, how and why we are the ones who know how to do it right, and to get anything right they need us, we are probably a big nitpicker. It's knee time. There was a need for hot pads to handle all the fire required to burn away all my issues, and a couple pair of knee-pads would have been helpful. This cleansing fire is still needed almost daily in my life. I'm sure that none of you are like that, right?

> For I am not ashamed of the gospel of Christ: for it is the power
> of God unto salvation to every one that believeth; to the Jew first,
> and also to the Greek.
>
> —ROMANS 1:16

If we are not walking in the power of the gospel of Christ, the power
of the Word of God, and the power Jesus said would come, how do
we think we are going to accomplish anything? The power is to equip
you to serve others and to save others. Most who have not done any
work for the kingdom of God do not understand that Satan is going to
try to stop them with many hindrances. We cannot do kingdom work
without kingdom power.

This may sound like something an advertising agency would come
up with: you can't do kingdom work without kingdom power! As I
have pointed out earlier, not many in the church (in fact I wonder how
many who may read this book) really understand Satan is the prince
of power of this world. Jesus did not send us power to stand idly by,
or to have to struggle our whole lives without succeeding. He sent us
the power of the Holy Ghost so we could accomplish His works. We
are to attain great and glorious achievements because of Jesus, as well
as for Jesus.

> Now is the judgment of this world: now shall the prince of this
> world be cast out. And I, if I be lifted up from the earth, will draw
> all men unto me.
>
> —JOHN 12:31–32

> Wherein in time past ye walked according to the course of this
> world, according to the prince of the power of the air, the spirit
> that now worketh in the children of disobedience.
>
> —EPHESIANS 2:2

A pastor once said in a sermon that when we are in the world as heathens, or sitting on a church pew doing nothing, we have no enemies.
You see, God is never our enemy and Satan will leave us alone as long as
we are doing Satan's work, or doing nothing at all. When we start doing
God's work, Satan will attack. Satan tempted Jesus and would like to

have Peter sifted as wheat. He will try to hinder us. Without knowing the power that God has given us, we will not succeed over Satan. It is all about our Father's business: souls! Satan wants yours and everyone else's he can get. We must know that before Jesus ascended, He told us He would send us power. However, if you do not understand or use the power, Satan has already won. The lack of this understanding and power is why so many churches are never fulfilling God's plans.

Jesus is not a deceiver, neither does He nor can He lie. As Jesus said, He is the way, the truth, and the life. (See John 14:6.) Jesus also said, "Destroy this temple and I will raise it up in three days," and He did. He also spoke to the winds and waves, saying "Peace be still" (Mark 4:39). Jesus also said:

> But ye shall receive power, after that the Holy Ghost is come upon you: and ye shall be witnesses unto me both in Jerusalem, and in all Judaea, and in Samaria, and unto the uttermost part of the earth.
>
> —ACTS 1:8

If Jesus said it, I am just going to believe it, and so should the churches. Without this power the churches are no threat to Satan, they are powerless, ineffective entities of the world. The biggest question in the church today must be: if Jesus sent this power, why are we not using it and being victorious? Instead, we are losing our neighborhoods, our very own children, and our nation to Satan.

The churches not using this power are not keeping one soul out of Satan's hands, and they are themselves spiritually dead. These churches are called by many names, but we could call them all zombie churches. They are the moving dead. Let's get very real here. They are in every town and of every denomination. Every living thing grows and multiplies itself. Do you know any churches that haven't grown and are not reproducing? They are the zombie churches. If you're in one, get out. The only change in these churches comes from the deaths and births of the zombie congregations.

> Behold, I give unto you power to tread on serpents and scorpions, and over all the power of the enemy: and nothing shall by

any means hurt you. Notwithstanding in this rejoice not, that the spirits are subject unto you; but rather rejoice, because your names are written in heaven.

—LUKE 10:19–20

If you do not know or believe you have power, if you do not know that every spirit of hell is subject to He that is in you, and that you are a son or daughter of the most high God, you need to be feeding and growing yourself. We must be complete ourselves before beginning to work on growing a pastor. We cannot give or teach what we do not have. Neither can we, nor a pastor, take others to where we have not been. An exception to the rule, that it is never to be about us, is here. This is where we must always put ourselves first. We must have the mind of Christ and the power of Christ in us before we can do anything for the kingdom of God. We can't grow a crop without being capable of tilling the soil and protecting it from the devourer.

For even Christ pleased not himself; but, as it is written, The reproaches of them that reproached thee fell on me.

—ROMANS 15:3

After being a good servant, this is probably the next important revelation we need to know. Kingdom works are never about us. That means they are not about me and they are not about you. It's not about what we want or how we think things should be. There are many churches and pastors who think that it must be done a certain way. For instance, many have preconceived ideals that worship can only be done just so, with the music set a certain way, or that we must dress a certain way, with the firm conviction that there is only one way to do anything. Why, and who said so? When we are not willing to change and move up towards God, and let the Holy Ghost have His way in our life and church services, we are being bound by a religious spirit. We all must seek a closer relationship with God and always be in the process of moving up. We have to leave where we are to get where He is. We must get this, every last one of us. We have to leave where we are to get closer to God. We must move, go, and grow if we are really seeking God! Moses had to go up to God, Jesus was lifted up to the right hand of the Father, and we must move up also to be in His presence.

The religious spirit is a powerful spirit. We need to remember it was the very spirit that opposed Christ during his earthly ministry and ultimately demanded that He be crucified. It takes prayer and fasting to break this demon's assignments. This demon will have a church dogmatically standing on some worthless principle, completely missing every move of God. There are important principles that we cannot move or bend on, and we do need to stand and then stand. However, we must remember and take to heart these verses also:

> For if any be a hearer of the word, and not a doer, he is like unto a man beholding his natural face in a glass: For he beholdeth himself, and goeth his way, and straightway forgetteth what manner of man he was. But whoso looketh into the perfect law of liberty, and continueth therein, he being not a forgetful hearer, but a doer of the work, this man shall be blessed in his deed. If any man among you seem to be religious, and bridleth not his tongue, but deceiveth his own heart, this man's religion is vain. Pure religion and undefiled before God and the Father is this, To visit the fatherless and widows in their affliction, and to keep himself unspotted from the world.
>
> —James 1:23–27

We must accept the simple fact that our churches must always be God's house of prayer. We are God's chosen people and we can only have a relationship in His presence if it's His way. Successful churches are those that allow the Holy Ghost to have His way. Every aspect, especially the pastor, is in subjection to the Holy Ghost. You must be grown to allow this in your life and church. Many churches are stagnant, dry, boring places, because they will not even consider that God's way is something different. When we get into His will for our lives and church, His spirit will be manifested in us.

It's sad to hear the name-calling and finger-pointing from some people and churches. If these people and churches were to look at themselves through the Word of God, most would see they have not expanded the kingdom of God one bit. They are quick to criticize churches that are successful because they don't do things "their way."

Many good, well-intentioned, and loving people are misguided and controlled by this demonic spirit of religion. They will not even consider the possibility that someone else's way could faintly be correct. Who's will do they think they are doing? We must start taking our churches back from Satan. Today, the greatest mission fields are in the churches. We must win them so we can win the world.

> For who hath known the mind of the Lord, that he may instruct him? but we have the mind of Christ.
> —1 CORINTHIANS 2:16

> Finally, be ye all of one mind, having compassion one of another, love as brethren, be pitiful, be courteous.
> —1 PETER 3:8

Here is where knowing who we are, what we can have, and what we can become will become evident. We are to have the mind of Christ, God said so. (See 1 Corinthians 2:16.) If we cannot believe this, how can we believe many of the other promises? It is all true, or none of it is true. We cannot trust that we have salvation without also trusting that every promise in the Bible is true. Jesus is either all truth or all lie, there is no in-between! We, as individuals as well as the church, must start by having and possessing everything God has already given us and start taking back everything Satan has stolen.

> Feed the flock of God which is among you, taking the oversight thereof, not by constraint, but willingly; not for filthy lucre, but of a ready mind; Neither as being lords over God's heritage, but being examples to the flock.
> —1 PETER 5:2–3

There are many pastors feeding their flock, not as Jesus would have us fed, but by their own way. When we are fed anything except God's Word, we become spiritually malnourished. The worldly teaching becomes apparent in us. When people see us, look at our works, and listen to our words, what example have we given them? Countless thousands do not attend church because when they visited they could not find God. We must realize many did not find God because God was not there. They actually have a better spirit of discernment than those in the churches. What does that tell us? If people cannot see past us and see Jesus in our lives, we are failing. We must be changed. If we are not changed, having died to ourselves, we are not of God and we are not saved. To repent means to turn away and stop doing the things that we know are wrong. So, let me say it again: if we have not changed, then we are not saved, nor are we born again. What many see when they visit our churches are the lost zombies, and they do not want to be a part of it.

How could we be a pastoral tree and fruit inspector for God if we are not even of God? Every person walking with God's Spirit should be set apart and different. If our light does not shine, then God's Spirit of light is not in us. To see the importance and reality of this all we need to do is look at Reverend Billy Graham. He is by far not the most exciting speaker. He has not given us any new revelations in the Scriptures. Yet without a doubt, he is one of the greatest soul-winners God has ever raised up. Why? Because people simply see clear through Reverend Graham and see the manifested presence of Jesus in him and in his words. That is the power of the Spirit of God. May God bless Reverend Graham. His rewards in heaven will be many.

We can get offended and mad, or we can grasp what is true. Our eternal life and those that we could save will depend on our choice. It's simple, read the Word of God and see what happens when we become a kingdom child, including what we are to have, how we are to act, and what we are to do. It is easy to find the answers; our heavenly Father has put them in His book just for us. Every test of God is always an open book test. We always have the answers!

> To open their eyes, and to turn them from darkness to light, and from the power of Satan unto God, that they may receive forgiveness of sins, and inheritance among them which are sanctified by faith that is in me.
>
> —ACTS 26:18

We are to be sanctified by faith in Jesus, set apart, living in this world but not of this world. Does our life represent us, or what Jesus did in us? Do our neighbors, our fellow workers, and every person we encounter know we are a Christian? The Samaritan woman who met Jesus at the well said, "Sir, I perceive that thou art a prophet" (John 4:19). Do people perceive we are Christians? When we are in a group, does the language and discussion change to what would be acceptable to speak in front of Jesus, or do we become one of them? If people do not stop swearing in our presence, we are not representing Jesus; our light is not shining. It's not us, it's the spirit of He that is in us, and most all people perceive when the Spirit of God is present. Every demon of hell knew who Jesus was, and if He is in us, they should also know who we are in Him.

I personally believe most just do not understand a very simple fact. Where there is light, darkness cannot be. The opposite is also true, there will be no light in the darkness. What do we think happens when we become the temple of God, which houses His very Spirit, and go to an R-rated or X-rated movie? What happens when we are standing in the presence of people using the Lord's name in vain or profanity? We are participating in, or at the least condoning, these acts of the spirit of darkness. Do we really think God turns His head for a few hours? Do we believe He really does not always hear what comes out of our mouths?

Can we make a mistake? Yes. Can we have a double standard and be both of the world and of God? No! It is time we have pastors preaching the truth that many of us are tithing double agents headed to hell. We need pastors who love and care enough for us to tell us the truth.

> I beseech you therefore, brethren, by the mercies of God, that ye present your bodies a living sacrifice, holy, acceptable unto God, which is your reasonable service. And be not conformed to this world: but be ye transformed by the renewing of your mind, that ye may prove what is that good, and acceptable, and perfect, will of God.
>
> —ROMANS 12:1–2

This is where truth is revealed, "where the rubber meets the road," that you may prove: does my life represent the perfect will of God, or my will? Most of us were grown in a school system. We were judged or graded on every aspect that seemed important by the school system. Normally, our day was divided into classes, and we were judged continually to see if we were in the will of the teachers and education system. What would our report card look like for our weekly, daily, or hourly classes of God's will? Many may receive an A when at Sunday school just to get an F at the workplace. Some may get an A for neighbor relations but fail in spousal relations. To make good grades in school we had to study and apply ourselves by learning the acceptable will of the school. The very same requirements apply to pass in the "acceptable will of God" course. The big difference here is that failure is eternal damnation. We must be in God's will before trying to grow others, whether they are family members or pastors. We can't even grow ourselves outside of the will of God.

Now that we have reviewed some of the criteria for the inspection of a pastor, let's see how and what we are to inspect. The *how* part is easy. We are to inspect with great reverence for the position the pastor holds. Inspections are to be done only in love and only by the Word of God. If we do not understand the difference between judging and inspecting, we must go to the Word and get it straight in our minds. The actions we are about to take will determine how we will be judged when we stand at the judgment bar of Christ. This is important stuff, and it is only for real, grown, brothers and sisters in Christ. If there is any motive to judge our pastors other than the love for God's kingdom and the love for our pastor, we will have to answer to God. If we hinder His chosen vessel instead of helping, we are simply doing Satan's work. We may burn in hell if we get this wrong, especially if we have the wrong motive. Besides having a correct motive, we must be able to withstand the fiery darts of the devil. He will want you even more at this point and will try to destroy your works. We must be sure to be in the will of God, in His authority!

The best instructions and the only instructions are to go forward and always make sure it is about Jesus and not about us or our feelings or agendas. Never back up. In other words, never give in to the devil! Never stop doing God's work! When we back up, or lose ground to Satan, we hinder God's work in us.

Go forward in God. It is important work. There are great pastors in small and large churches that are doing God's work and need help: they need spiritual help, physical help, and help sharing the load. There are also pastors in many churches leading unsuspecting people to hell. We, as individuals and as the body of Christ, have much to do and time is limited. It will start to be accomplished when I do my part, joined by you doing your part, and then we together do our part. As a result, God's plan will come to fruition.

What are we to do? We must first see that only the Word of God is being preached and taught in our churches. Here is where no flexibility can exist, and I do not care who your pastor is, or how big your church is, or what particular denomination it is. Your pastor may be on television or radio and may have articles in many publications and be seen as having one of the greatest ministries ever to be. However, if what he speaks and does are not based on God's Word, it all is not of God. We should discern that most media companies are really instruments of Satan. This is easily discerned by their presented format. If anything other than the Holy Bible, which is the inspired Word of God, is being taught, stop it. It is of Satan and not of God. Do not be confused by some church book or doctrine. There is one God and only one book. "Almost," "close to," and "going to be" do not count, and anything less than the whole Word of God must not be found in our churches.

> For there are many unruly and vain talkers and deceivers, specially they of the circumcision: Whose mouths must be stopped, who subvert whole houses, teaching things which they ought not, for filthy lucre's sake. One of themselves, even a prophet of their own, said, The Cretians are always liars, evil beasts, slow bellies. This witness is true. Wherefore rebuke them sharply, that they may be sound in the faith; Not giving heed to Jewish fables, and commandments of men, that turn from the truth. Unto the pure all things are pure: but unto them that are defiled and unbelieving is nothing pure; but even their mind and conscience is defiled. They profess that they know God; but in works they deny him, being abominable, and disobedient, and unto every good work reprobate.
>
> —TITUS 1:10–16

That we henceforth be no more children, tossed to and fro, and carried about with every wind of doctrine, by the sleight of men, and cunning craftiness, whereby they lie in wait to deceive; But speaking the truth in love, may grow up into him in all things, which is the head, even Christ.

—EPHESIANS 4:14–15

Whosoever transgresseth, and abideth not in the doctrine of Christ, hath not God. He that abideth in the doctrine of Christ, he hath both the Father and the Son. If there come any unto you, and bring not this doctrine, receive him not into your house, neither bid him God speed: For he that biddeth him God speed is partaker of his evil deeds.

—2 JOHN 1:9–11

In the beginning of this book, I emphasized that we must read before and after a scripture to know that we are getting the true meaning. Please research the above scriptures (and others that you read). You'll find we were warned about what is happening in our churches. There are many large denominations that simply have added to the Bible, added a little of Jesus here and there to appear to be in line with God, but really teach a false doctrine. They are all being deceived, and they are serving Satan. They will all burn in hell according to the real Word of God. We must know we are not a part of this.

God spoke through prophets most of the time. When He spoke directly to the people it was always of great importance. Jehovah God knew the ending from the beginning and gave us prophets and the Bible to show us what was going to happen and why. Often, we do not hear God when He speaks to us, and we fail miserably in our prayer lives.

Father, glorify thy name. Then came there a voice from heaven, saying, I have both glorified it, and will glorify it again. The people therefore, that stood by, and heard it, said that it thundered: others said, An angel spake to him. Jesus answered and said, This voice came not because of me, but for your sakes.

—JOHN 12:28–30

We need to wake up every day looking for the coming of our Lord. God has glorified Him and is going to glorify Him again. When we see Him coming, in that instant, it will be too late for many. His first visit from heaven to earth was as a Lamb to be slain. When that cloud appears in the sky and a light like we have never seen shines behind it, then we will see Jesus as the Lion of the tribe of Judah. He is Jehovah—He who was, He who is, and He who will be. I believe anybody who makes Jesus anything less than what He is will find the wrath of God more so than any others. Jesus paid a price, God gave a sacrificial gift in love. To add or take away from this work means you will surely burn in hell.

> And if any man shall take away from the words of the book of this prophecy, God shall take away his part out of the book of life, and out of the holy city, and from the things which are written in this book. He which testifieth these things saith, Surely I come quickly. Amen. Even so, come, Lord Jesus. The grace of our Lord Jesus Christ be with you all. Amen.
>
> —REVELATION 22:19–21

This is the inspired Word of God. And according to God, the two fastest growing churches in the United States, the Mormon church and the Jehovah's Witnesses, are lost to an eternal hell. They are wonderful, great, loving people, however, they are deceived to damnation because they have added and taken away from God's Word. Jesus was not just another prophet, though Jesus was a great prophet, He is the Christ and the only way to the Father. There are no other books, plaques, or tablets from God, simply and surely because God said so.

There is a price to be paid when we do not reverence God's possessions. Every pastor called by God is His. Every church building and sanctuary is His. Think about this: Jesus, having been scourged, spat upon, beaten, and nailed to a cross, said these words:

> Then said Jesus, Father, forgive them; for they know not what they do. And they parted his raiment, and cast lots.
>
> —LUKE 23:34

Consider Jesus' attitude towards God's house as a house of prayer, when He reacted to the moneychangers:

> And Jesus went into the temple of God, and cast out all them that sold and bought in the temple, and overthrew the tables of the moneychangers, and the seats of them that sold doves, And said unto them, It is written, My house shall be called the house of prayer; but ye have made it a den of thieves.
>
> —MATTHEW 21:12–13

What has happened to God's houses? We have decided it's okay to sell, it's for a good cause, it's "Churchy Stuff." Jesus didn't ask for them to be forgiven, and he used a scourge. We must really get a grasp on what is important to God, based on His Word and not how we want things today. We have interpreted that, yes, it was wrong for the money changers, but it is okay for us. What scripture do we use, how in God's name do we think our cause is different? God has not and will not change. How many scriptures have we ignored and altered just like the pagans, scribes, and Pharisees did? By deceiving ourselves that it is now okay, we believe that we are somehow different and God will allow us.

> For I am the LORD, I change not; therefore ye sons of Jacob are not consumed.
>
> —MALACHI 3:6

We as a society of individuals and churches have changed to today's morality by the winds of our time and we expect God to meet us there. He will not. We have to go back to God. Popularity and majorities have never moved God, in fact, history indicates God prefers remnants.

Now, as never before, we need real pastors who are mighty men of God and will stand for what they believe in. Thank God, there are some. Sadly, more than ever before, pastors are leaving the pulpits at an alarming rate. This is not acceptable and should not be happening in our churches. I want to speak to those pastors. First, if you're leaving the ministry because you realized you were not really called of God, leave and may God bless whatever venture you enter into. You should be one of the best servants in the church you attend. There are many people who are not ministers but are still making a big difference for God. They are the sons and daughters of the most high God. They are simply in a family relationship with the Father, Son, and Holy Ghost. That should now be your place, and you should be treated accordingly, with understanding and love, as well as reverence for the sacrifice you were willing to make.

If you were called by God and there were no people to help "grow you" and support you until you were mature in Christ, I'm sorry. I truly wish that we as the body of Christ had treated you better. I hope this book will bring awareness to the needs and real difficulties young pastors have, along with the need for Christians to accept the responsibility to help. However, in the love of Christ, I must speak to you by the Word of God.

> And Jesus said unto him, No man, having put his hand to the plough, and looking back, is fit for the kingdom of God.
> —LUKE 9:62

You quitters better understand this: you are not fit to enter the kingdom of God; that is according to Jesus, who is the only door to the kingdom of God. I would like to make a suggestion to those who used to be ministers. Write down all of your problems, such as why you left the ministry, the pain, suffering, and disappointments. When you have compiled your list and your difficulties, review these men called of God and their ministries: Job, Moses, Daniel, Jacob, even Noah. Many mighty men in our pulpits today had to fight Satan every inch of the way. Get on your knees, repent, pick yourself up and go on, not as some poor, defeated orphan, but as a chosen child of God. Your were chosen at a special time in history, you have a part to do and God has not changed His mind. God's plan for you may be to start the next great revival that ushers in Jesus. Whatever it is, if you allow God to use you, and you use God, His goal for you will be reached. Out of countless millions you were chosen by Jehovah, how can you fail? It is impossible! You are God's, the work you are to do is God's, and it is up to God's capabilities. As soon as you're off your knees, go to work. I need you, we need you, the world needs you, God needs you. Help us, please!

> And because ye are sons, God hath sent forth the Spirit of his Son into your hearts, crying, Abba, Father. Wherefore thou art no more a servant, but a son; and if a son, then an heir of God through Christ. Howbeit then, when ye knew not God, ye did service unto them which by nature are no gods. But now, after that ye have known God, or rather are known of God, how turn ye again to the weak and beggarly elements, whereunto ye desire again to be in bondage?
> —GALATIANS 4:6–9

We must settle a very important question in our hearts, actually, it's more a position or choice. Do we want to fight Satan in this day and time, knowing He that is in us is greater than he who is in the world? Or do we want to spend eternity with Satan? Jesus has already won the battle for us. Whatever we know, we must know that Satan loses. If we are allowing a loser to beat us, it's not because he is better, it is simply that we do not know who we are and who we serve. Find a pastor fighting the good fight and winning, ask him to lay hands on you and anoint you with the power God has for you. Hey, don't be stupid! It's not about you. It's about He that is in you. It's His power and authority. It's only about your obedience. Stop trusting in your abilities, they are not good enough. God did not call you to lose. Get up and go kick some demons around just because you can.

Mighty pastors are going be preaching the Word of God and preparing us to meet Jesus. They must stand on God's Word, and we must stand with them. Look at our churches, our country, our schools, and our neighbors who have all been made to be of little or no effect by Satan. We must win them back. Not by being popular, nor should we worry that we might offend someone. We better be worrying about offending God. We are either for or against Him. There is no other position. If Jesus were to return this day, would our lives, our works, and our fruits clearly show we were for Jesus? When we should have taken a stand, did we stand? Where are the pastors who are still standing? Where will we get more like them?

Abortion is wrong. It's not about women's rights. It's about an inno-cent life. It's a choice about convenience. How could a Christian nation have such a position? How did we the church allow this to happen? What part of judgment will we have to account for? We buy products, watch television, and listen to radio stations all supporting a lifestyle that has been designed by Satan himself. Stop! It's our money that is being used to destroy our Christian way of life.

Divorce is wrong. The church should be setting an example, yet divorce in the church is no less than that of the heathens in this world. What does that tell us? We need to be supporting families and cou-ples by giving them the tools to succeed. It's time we understand it's not about our happiness or our feelings, it's about the Word of God and should be about the children. Divorce is going from generation to generation destroying our children and grandchildren. It's become normal, so normal that many in the pulpit are divorced. The sad part is it's so easy to stop. Put God first, put our spouses before us, and be the wife or husband God tells us to be. Well, it can't be that simple! It is. The day a person truly puts God first and their spouse ahead of them-selves is the day God will bless their marriage and rebuke Satan out of their family. Where are our leaders? We must be raising them up fast.

We have instruments that measure time to a minute fraction of a second over thousands of years. It is, I'm sure, wonderful technology, however a waste as Jesus will return long before it will ever be ben-eficial. However, I want to share with you a revelation God gave me. Beside the natural time we function in, there is a spiritual time. Spiri-tual time is under the same law of God as gravity. When an object falls, its rate of speed doubles every second until it reaches the maximum speed possible, being affected by worldly resistance. Jesus' return will be determined by spiritual time, not natural time. As the time for Jesus' return approaches, spiritual events will gain speed The same holds true for those who have fallen to Satan's deceptions. Just like gravity they will begin to fall faster and faster. Our nation is now in the fallen state of spiritual time. This is very evident in the changes over just the last few years. We will begin to fall faster and faster. We need pastors who will be like Isaiah and ask God to turn back time, and God will!

And Hezekiah said unto Isaiah, What shall be the sign that the LORD will heal me, and that I shall go up into the house of the LORD the third day? And Isaiah said, This sign shalt thou have of the LORD, that the LORD will do the thing that he hath spoken: shall the shadow go forward ten degrees, or go back ten degrees? And Hezekiah answered, It is a light thing for the shadow to go down ten degrees: nay, but let the shadow return backward ten degrees. And Isaiah the prophet cried unto the LORD: and he brought the shadow ten degrees backward, by which it had gone down in the dial of Ahaz.

—2 KINGS 20:8–11

Look at the work of these pastors. We have been given that the gay and lesbian lifestyle is a normal, alternate way of life that is to be accepted. It's not acceptable, it's from hell. We as a church, need to be delivering these people from Satan's grasp and not condoning their behavior. It's a sin and, like any other sin, we need to speak out and denounce it. We need to be expressing our real love to the homosexual community, but not tolerate their sin or claim it is anything but sin. Let us not single out this sin, it is no different than divorce, lying, gossiping, or even just thinking lustful thoughts. If it were not for mercy, every one of us would be sent to an eternal hell.

We allowed a few uneducated idiots to take prayer out of our schools and look at what has happened. We have shootings, drugs, sex, and no respect for God or any authority. The ten commandants and prayer have been removed and replaced by police officers patrolling the hallways, fending off the drug dealers. With the removal of the Ten Commandments, there is an opening for Satan to get in! This is happening even at our grade schools. We hear time and time again that things are so bad because it is just the times, not because we have forsaken our God. That is a lie straight from hell and shows how we are losing the war with Satan. That spiritual time is just doubling and doubling! God, please give us some real and godly pastors soon!

We must understand that we are no longer a nation under God, but a nation against God. The United States of America now has no place for God. He is not allowed into any government building, including our schools. Every one of us voted, even ignored and allowed this to happen. We were too comfortable, too busy, too involved with our own wants and wishes. We, as a nation, are paying the price for this with the lives and souls of our children. We are responsible, and we must have righteous pastors to lead us back to God.

We are at a time when so many churches and pastors are trying to do God's work without God. It's also time that when a man or woman takes a stand with God against Satan's works, they no longer need to stand alone. We must join forces. We must support those who are standing up for God's will. We must stand with pastors who are leading their flock toward God and by God. We must be about growing more of these pastors. Where are they going to come from? Who is going to grow them?

Chapter Five

TREES OF ENDURANCE

Spiritually maturing, growing, and fruit-producing pastoral trees will need care their entire lives. These are our pastors that are on the front lines evangelizing the world, as well as those that are simply feeding their small flocks in Somewhereville, USA. They all need our care. An appropriate name for these trees would be "trees of long-suffering." Some may only require seasonal care and some full-time care.

Let's first start with the small churches or small flocks being fed all over the world. I believe these bodies of Christ are just as important, if not more so, to Jesus than the mega-churches we have today. There are no great and small souls, none more important than any other. The size of the tree is never mentioned in the Bible, just the importance of the fruit.

> For if the firstfruit be holy, the lump is also holy: and if the root be holy, so are the branches. And if some of the branches be broken off, and thou, being a wild olive tree, wert graffed in among them, and with them partakest of the root and fatness of the olive tree; Boast not against the branches. But if thou boast, thou bearest not the root, but the root thee. Thou wilt say then, The branches were broken off, that I might be graffed in.
>
> —ROMANS 11:16–19

103

What wonderful verses! The root is God, and we are the branches that were grafted in. We, the Gentiles, are described as the wild olive tree. One look at the state of our morality, wild is probably not fitting. By the grace and mercy of God, we are to be partakers of the root and the fatness of God. We sure need to appreciate without measure this wonderful gift and understand the importance of offering our first fruits. We, being branches of the living God, must then be producing fruit and offering up our firstfruits. When we see unproductive churches, it is clear to see they must not be grafted to the root of God.

The smaller churches are able to change more easily without any rigid doctrine or man-made denominational restrictions. These churches simply appear closer to the root of God in many cases. We must be very careful in larger churches. Some have branches that have grown too far from the root. In growing away from the root of God, we quickly start turning rapidly back into the wild olive branches. We have witnessed the tragedies that have happened and continue to happen in our larger denominations. We need to be in prayer for all churches, especially the mega-churches, who being so large and well-financed could be changing the world for the glory of God. God has given us everything we need to be great producers, and we will when we come together and work together.

There have been some mighty servants of God that have been raised up out of small churches. It is important to realize that, though size is not important, a church without growth cannot be a healthy church, nor can a church without all age groups be healthy. Every healthy tree will have buds, leaves, blossoms, and fruit.

> The wilderness and the solitary place shall be glad for them; and the desert shall rejoice, and blossom as the rose. It shall blossom abundantly, and rejoice even with joy and singing: the glory of Lebanon shall be given unto it, the excellency of Carmel and Sharon, they shall see the glory of the LORD, and the excellency of our God. Strengthen ye the weak hands, and confirm the feeble knees. Say to them that are of a fearful heart, Be strong, fear not: behold, your God will come with vengeance, even God with a recompence; he will come and save you. Then the eyes of the blind shall be opened, and the ears of the deaf shall be unstopped. Then

shall the lame man leap as an hart, and the tongue of the dumb sing: for in the wilderness shall waters break out, and streams in the desert. And the parched ground shall become a pool, and the thirsty land springs of water: in the habitation of dragons, where each lay, shall be grass with reeds and rushes. And an highway shall be there, and a way, and it shall be called The way of holiness; the unclean shall not pass over it; but it shall be for those: the wayfaring men, though fools, shall not err therein. No lion shall be there, nor any ravenous beast shall go up thereon, it shall not be found there; but the redeemed shall walk there.

—ISAIAH 35:1–9

These are the blossoms and fruit that the roots of God will grow. Praise God that they shall blossom abundantly. The church is full of healing, it will be the way of holiness, and the unclean shall not pass. It is for the wayfaring men, those that fear and are obedient to God. This is God's Word and His desire for us to have.

We certainly understand and appreciate the small church in the small rural towns across America. There are, however, too many small churches that are convinced "small" is all they can ever be. Their mindset is: small building, small town, poor part of town, it has always been this way and always will be. Unfortunately, our pastors get caught up in this. They feel limited, even defeated, and do not reach their full potential or God's will for their lives. I have no idea what God's plans are for any church other than those spoken in His Word. But I do know there are no natural limitations of God, only man. If God can send manna and quail to the desert, He can send congregations to any church. If God said He would add to the church daily, why do we not just believe it?

Many times this grows upon a pastor and congregation just like a life-sucking vine does on a tree. This vine represents many different burdens placed upon the church and pastor. The vine grows just a little daily, just a little more each year, until the tree is covered in nothing but vines. The tree itself is now dead. It is now just a shell for something else. How many of our churches are just church-shaped shells that haven't produced any fruit for a long time?

We must ask: when was the last time there were salvations? Are people being saved and baptized on any regular basis? If not, what is the purpose of the church? If our answer is that there are twenty or thirty people still meeting on a regular basis, we still hold services, and we love and enjoy our services, then we need to understand that this is not a church in any spiritual sense. It has become a club, and a social club at that. This condition exists all across our nation. It is in all denominations and some more so than others. These congregations are made up of good people who had good intentions, and may have perfected and performed seemingly good services. Most of the time the services are very religious and structured with little or no flexibility and no freedom. The members have become so accustomed to the same people and the same seats, that they truly do not want new people coming and changing things. It happened so slowly and was unnoticed, until there was nothing but a shell. There was no decision to become this way, it just became a slow progression toward an unnoticed death. The church became something besides a body of Christ.

These religious strongholds are a result of the demonic spirit of religion and will be difficult to reach. They are happy people, giving God their hour and fifteen minutes every week. They attend all the social events, which are often, and they like it this way. It is all about what they like. The only way to reach them is going to be by great pastors being rebirthed and becoming true trees of Christ. I believe God is about to start a new and wonderful work in His chosen pastors. A fire is going to break out among pastors. The pastors of these churches need to get with those that are burning with the fire of God. These "on fire" pastors then need to take the fire back to their churches. These are important churches, which must not be forgotten by our large or "mega-church" mentality. We are now starting to see pastors, who have the fire and anointing of God, inviting other pastors to come and share. Pastors start going to these conferences, receiving all God has, and begin giving back into congregations and towns.

I hope some of our gifted pastors and speakers doing huge events will remember the thousands in these small-town churches. Follow the example of Jesus! He taught to multitudes, and also to the single woman at the well. The whole town came to Christ as a result of preaching to one. Maybe it is time these huge evangelists get off their

Lear jets and get on a Greyhound. Jesus rode a borrowed ass to Jerusalem to die for our sins as well as theirs. We must not forget the one or the few, Jesus didn't. Every revival of God has broken out of a small church, a small group, and God has always worked with remnants.

I want to give honor where honor is due. I am commanded to do so in the Scriptures. One of the greatest soul-winning evangelists of our time is Dwight Thompson. He is seen regularly on most Christian television stations, and on many programs. He speaks at huge churches and events and is always in demand. I was recently blessed to hear him minister for a three-day event. This event was for a very small church in a rented cafeteria of a public school. Some nights there were less than sixty people there. Dwight Thompson not only came to minister to a small congregation, but was just as enthused and anointed as when he preaches to millions on television. That is how great, obedient men of God are. May God continue to bless him, his ministry, and family greatly.

We need to provide the time and resources so that pastors of every church can meet together, not just at denominational meetings. Those are, however, very important also. We need our pastors meeting, fellowshipping, sharing, praying, and worshiping together. Praise God, tear down those old barriers, get together and fellowship, share, pray, catch something that will be contagious and will be of the one and only most high God. When you get back, you will be pulling down all those old vines from getting dunged and digged. There will be fruit produced. These pastors will greatly share in changing our country. It's doesn't have to just be the "mega-church" pastors being beamed around the world. It may be your church, it may be you personally, and it maybe your pastor that the next great revival will break out from.

If this vine-covered condition is our church, we must recognize our condition and simply want to change. This change will come only out of a love and desire for others, and not from what we want for ourselves. We all know who we are. We want access to the pastor at any time, and we need to know everyone and their business. We actually feel uncomfortable if a stranger, an outsider, is to accidentally show up at one of our services. It would be an accident because we have not invited anyone to our church for a long time. We act pleasant in our religious manner and, because of old habits formed long ago, we make sure any visitors are treated very well. Our true attitude and feelings are so evident that we never see visitors more than once or twice. We have also, in our still-religious manner, let the pastor know that we like it this way. We are the ones that are paying the bills and we should get what we like. It's our money, it's our church, and we should get it our way, right? We know that sometimes the shoe fits on the feet of many and not just one. To some extent this is each one of us and every church. Strong pastors are needed to fix this, and they are needed now.

That good "on-fire" pastor that showed up a few years ago has now become just like the congregation—spiritually dead! He or she is no more a lively tree, but just a shell. Life is easy! Please a few people, give them the sermon they want to hear, perform a wedding here, a funeral there, and life goes on and goes on easily. They thank God for blessing them. The congregation is happy, bills are being paid, and life is good. If the pastors are pleasing their flocks, and the flock is happy, they are fulfilling their calling, right? It all just happened so easily. Somehow, somewhere the fire has all but gone out, memories and thoughts of a great harvest may still exist, but it all seems far away and it must be for others to do.

These pastors used to hear the voice of God so clearly, but instead followed the voice of the people. They have ignored that small, still voice for so long that it has stopped speaking. Those dreams of revivals, church planting, preparing for multi-services, being asked to be a guest speaker, and doing evangelism and missionary work aren't even dreams anymore. These pastors must also ask themselves when was the last time they were leading someone in the sinner's prayer for the first time? When was the last baptism? More important than that, when did God speak to them last? When was the last time they truly obeyed God's will and not their own? Pastors and churches, when you meet Jesus, what do you believe His first words to you will be?

> His lord said unto him, Well done, good and faithful servant; thou hast been faithful over a few things, I will make thee ruler over many things: enter thou into the joy of thy lord.
>
> —MATTHEW 25:23

Churches and pastors get caught up in the lie from hell that God is pruning the church when attendance starts to drop. But there is a problem when any church is not growing. It's almost always a spiritual problem. Successful churches are growing in numbers as well as in spiritual growth. I have tried to stress that we always need to know God's Word and have faith that it's true. I have been in a church with dwindling numbers. It was one of the most difficult times of my life. The pain still exists. Thank God He excommunicated me right to a pastor that has a heart for evangelism and a great passion for the lost. My former pastor kept saying that God was pruning the church and getting rid of those with demonic spirits. If you have attended several churches you probably have experienced this, as it is widespread. It is a lie made up to cover up the shortcomings of both the pastor and church. The truth is that God will prune on the last day of judgment, and, until that day, we need to follow Jesus' lead. We will cast out the demons, and we will love the sinners to repentance. The act of people leaving a true blood-bought church will never be an act of God, but the failure of man. God cares for all to stay. In fact, He said, leave the ninety-nine and go after the one. (See Luke 15:4.) If you are in a church like this, the pain is almost unbearable to see the decay and deadness around you. It will almost always be covered up with programs, socials, and all types of "churchy" stuff. When confronted head on, these pastors will invariably say we need to go back to the basics that worked years ago. This is another lie. Get help for any pastor that wants to go back to what worked years ago. Christ is coming! We need to go forward, not backward! Here is where strong elders and deacons need to get involved in helping their pastors. Perhaps they should send the pastor where it is working and let them meet with those that have the answers. When it is working according to God's plan, He will add to the church. If the pastor is not willing to change and get it right, get one that will. Souls are dying and going to hell, it is time to prepare to meet our Lord, not prepare for another chicken dinner.

> And they, continuing daily with one accord in the temple, and breaking bread from house to house, did eat their meat with gladness and singleness of heart, Praising God, and having favour

with all the people. And the Lord added to the church daily such
as should be saved.

—Acts 2:46–47

The Church was doing their part and God did His part. This is a real
Christian church in correct operation of God's will and law. When it is
not God's way, we always hear the lie that God is pruning the church.
Please beware, Satan is close at hand. Again, the words "prune" and
"pruned" are only used three times in the whole Bible. Here they are,
keep them handy in case you ever hear those awful, dreaded words. I
do not want to be redundant but I want you to remember this unacceptable lie from hell.

> Six years thou shalt sow thy field, and six years thou shalt prune
> thy vineyard, and gather in the fruit thereof; But in the seventh
> year shall be a sabbath of rest unto the land, a sabbath for the
> Lord: thou shalt neither sow thy field, nor prune thy vineyard.
>
> —Leviticus 25:3–4

> And I will lay it waste: it shall not be pruned, nor digged; but
> there shall come up briers and thorns: I will also command the
> clouds that they rain no rain upon it.
>
> —Isaiah 5:6

Look at what God said, "Prune thy vineyard, and gather in the fruit
thereof." This is the Word of God. How is it then that every failure of
church growth has been labeled as "God's pruning the church"? People make excuses for a spiritual lack by trying to claim it's an act of
God. When we don't have the Word of God in us, we accept a lie as
truth. The truth is that healthy, godly churches will always be growing.
Unhealthy churches are never of God and will be dying. Be merciful
and follow Jesus' recommendation:

> And he answering said unto him, Lord, let it alone this year also,
> till I shall dig about it, and dung it: And if it bear fruit, well: and
> if not, then after that thou shalt cut it down.
>
> —Luke 13:8–9

We must supply the time and resources to correct a dying church. Yes, that may mean some of our money is needed. The change needed is simply and always to become like Christ and follow the Word of God. Now matter what the conditions, no matter where the church is, no matter how long it has been that way, the very second it becomes Christ's body of believers and doing it God's way, it will become alive again.

> But we all, with open face beholding as in a glass the glory of the Lord, are changed into the same image from glory to glory, even as by the Spirit of the Lord.
> —2 CORINTHIANS 3:18

It is that simple and will happen that quickly. We must simply do it His way. Let's ask ourselves, are we doing the things Christ did and those He commanded us to do? We all seek, and all of us in our hearts want to see miracles performed by Jesus. Besides salvation, the birth of life, whether a person or church, is one of the greatest miracles and is often overlooked. Either a person or church is dead or dying, yet the instant they turn to and accept God's plan, miraculously they become alive and can instantly produce fruit.

> Beloved, now are we the sons of God, and it doth not yet appear what we shall be: but we know that, when he shall appear, we shall be like him; for we shall see him as he is.
> —1 JOHN 3:2

We are now sons and daughters, and we shall be like Him. But are we?

Today, did we do as Jesus would have done? If you feel this is not the case, and you want to become and do what God has prepared, planned, and preordained from the very beginning of time, you still can. It's time for prayer, sound preaching, and coming together as the body of Christ to be and to do His will. Call a fast of the church, call an evangelist to come and relight that fire. Pastors, go to somebody's church that is "on fire," grab a hold of that pastor and simply say, "I'm not letting go until you pray for me, fill me with desire, fill me with fire, and bless me with everything God has for me. Help me find God. You know the way!"

Now the previous described condition of a church and pastor can only occur by improper pastoral growth, unacceptable growing conditions, and improper pruning. In every case, regardless of age, reasons, and excuses, the pastor must be responsible for he is the head. When there are men and women who truly care for God, their church, and their pastor, and who are knowledgeable in the Word of God, this will never happen. Please know the Word, know the Word, and then really know the Word. It is a must for every real and serious Christian. Go back and review the previous chapters on what needs to be pruned, and in Jesus' name start cutting. Sometimes a loving kick in the seat can do miracles. It is also hard to overfertilize with desire, emotions, love, enthusiasm, and encouragement. You can also not over-prune when pruning away the wants and needs of the worldly and the entrapments of the "my way" congregation. Remember always who is responsible, YOU are.

All pastors and all churches need to remember:

> And he gave some, apostles; and some, prophets; and some, evangelists; and some, pastors and teachers; For the perfecting of the saints, for the work of the ministry, for the edifying of the body of Christ: Till we all come in the unity of the faith, and of the knowledge of the Son of God, unto a perfect man, unto the measure of the stature of the fulness of Christ: That we henceforth be no more children, tossed to and fro, and carried about with every wind of doctrine, by the sleight of men, and cunning craftiness, whereby they lie in wait to deceive; But speaking the truth in love, may grow up into him in all things, which is the head, even Christ.
>
> —EPHESIANS 4:11–15

The truth is, most pastors do not walk in the complete fivefold ministry. God never intended them to be all things all the time, and we cannot expect them to be. We must invite others in who are called by God to their respective offices. They will carry a strong anointing in their offices. Without them in our churches at appointed times, our churches will never be complete. I do not know of one successful pastor who does not bring in those who are more gifted in other areas to help feed his flock. It's all about growth; not ours, but the kingdom of God's. The pastor who is afraid to bring in highly gifted people is walking in the flesh and the spirit of jealously. This needs to be pruned. However, before we start pruning the pastor, has your church given him liberty, encouragement, and confidence, or fear of losing his job? The truth is, even without knowing it, we are all growing our pastors. Was your pastor grown in love and understanding, or did he really receive just a whole bunch of dung? Many churches are great on the dung but short on the digging.

A confident man or woman of God will not be threatened by those that are more gifted. They will want to learn and be fed just like the rest of us. One of the smartest pastors I have had the privilege of knowing is Pastor Johnny Jordon. He is the pastor of a growing African-American church in Apopka, Florida, the St. Elisabeth's Praise and Worship Center. He has great men and women of God come to speak at his church. At a time when he could be heard by many from the pulpit, he is found sitting down, being fed. I have a great respect for this man and continue to learn from him. He knows how to be smart. Maybe you do not need this, but I do. We all need to know when we need to be fed—not only us, but our pastors. This is how we grow. How are you growing your pastor?

This is important! Again, I may make some angry, but I believe it is so true. If you are saved and truly born again with Jesus in you, you will understand the value of a lost soul. If we understand and truly know that value, as well as God's will, all things will be about saving the lost and will never be about us. So if the subject or topic is all about you in your expectations of your pastor, you may be one of those being deceived and headed to hell. If so, and you are reading this, you can get mad or get right. It's a choice. Has your choice brought you what God said it would? If not, find out why and do it before it is too late.

We need to have a salvation rededication day, complete with baptisms for the whole church body across this nation. It would be a special day of fasting and prayer dedicating ourselves, our pastors, and our churches to the one and true God. This day would also include time for repentance for our failures and inactivity. The result would be for the whole body of Christ to find a shared and unified vision of the future of the Father's business. We all say we want a revival of our churches and our nation; here would be a great start. Revival of our churches, pastors, and ourselves would start and spread across this land crossing every denominational line.

> But the fruit of the Spirit is love, joy, peace, longsuffering, gentleness, goodness, faith, meekness, temperance: against such there is no law. And they that are Christ's have crucified the flesh with the affections and lusts. If we live in the Spirit, let us also walk in the Spirit. Let us not be desirous of vain glory, provoking one another, envying one another.
> —GALATIANS 5:22–26

These are not just some words, they are God's Words! They are His promises, and they are true. If we are not living them and fulfilling them, there must be a problem. There are two options to the problem: either God's Words or us. We must keep in mind that in our lives, as well as trying to help grow a pastor, things will take time. If we are not growing, we must find the answer why. This truth applies to individuals as pastors and as the body of Christ. There must be growth. We must be producing. If there is no spiritual fruit and no salvations, the works are clearly not of God. We must always quickly know when there is a problem or a shortcoming that, first and foremost, it's not God. We must be looking in the mirror to see the problem. The very first person to look at to fix the problem should always be *me*. If we had daily self-examinations and love in our hearts, we could be in and of a church that is winning the lost. Love, in a real body of Christ, is a love for the lost, not just for the family and friends we have inside those four walls that we have now deemed a church. Church is where the lost are! Where the sick are! Where the hurting are! That is a church after God's heart. When we get this we will be doing what Jesus did, instead of what we now think church is. Go! Go! And send!

Jesus the Christ died for us. He showed us His love as well as told us of the importance of love. These are His words! How important do you think a growing, fruit-producing church is to Him?

> He spake also this parable; A certain man had a fig tree planted in his vineyard; and he came and sought fruit thereon, and found none. Then said he unto the dresser of his vineyard, Behold, these three years I come seeking fruit on this fig tree, and find none: cut it down; why cumbereth it the ground? And he answering said unto him, Lord, let it alone this year also, till I shall dig about it, and dung it: And if it bear fruit, well: and if not, then after that thou shalt cut it down.
>
> —LUKE 13:6–9

How long have you been a Christian? How long did Jesus give us in this parable to bear fruit? Ladies and gentleman, this is real stuff, we are to be about the Father's business. We should be enthusiastic about serving God and saving souls. The same old, same old will take us to hell.

> I know thy works, that thou art neither cold nor hot: I would thou wert cold or hot. So then because thou art lukewarm, and neither cold nor hot, I will spue thee out of my mouth. Because thou sayest, I am rich, and increased with goods, and have need of nothing; and knowest not that thou art wretched, and miserable, and poor, and blind, and naked: I counsel thee to buy of me gold tried in the fire, that thou mayest be rich; and white raiment, that thou mayest be clothed, and that the shame of thy nakedness do not appear; and anoint thine eyes with eyesalve, that thou mayest see. As many as I love, I rebuke and chasten: be zealous therefore, and repent.
>
> —REVELATION 3:15–19

These words were spoken with the same love that was given at the cross. We should therefore heed them with great care. They were spoken for many, if not all, of us. It seems in our demanding world it is easy to leave out of our schedule the most important works we will ever be given. We must pray for mercy and ask for God's help. Without mercies, we will all surely perish to hell.

We must be hot for Jesus, hot with passion for the lost! We are the last-day church, born at such a time as this and for a reason. As we examine ourselves, our local church, and our pastor we need to get real. We need to get real with the will of Christ and consumed with the righteousness of God. Look at your church, look at its programs and budgets. The real truth will be there. What did you and your church do and spend to reach the lost? If there aren't any toes I haven't yet stepped on, I will here. The vast majority of churches spent more on ridiculous Christmas and Easter programs than on reaching the lost. While there are many churches who have effective seasonal programs at Christmas and Easter, winning the lost to Christ, many do not, focusing instead on themes that merely entertain instead of evangelize. How in God's name did we ever get the command to do this out of the Scriptures? If you're a Christian, you must know the Word of God says the angels rejoice when a lost soul is saved. How many angels are rejoicing over our absurd programs? It is just entertainment and no different than going to a movie. We just try to claim it is important. Yes, it is to us, but not to God. We confuse worship with some music and words. True worship starts with obedience to our Lord.

> And why call ye me, Lord, Lord, and do not the things which I say? Whosoever cometh to me, and heareth my sayings, and doeth them, I will shew you to whom he is like: He is like a man which built an house, and digged deep, and laid the foundation on a rock: and when the flood arose, the stream beat vehemently upon that house, and could not shake it: for it was founded upon a rock. But he that heareth, and doeth not, is like a man that without a foundation built an house upon the earth; against which the stream did beat vehemently, and immediately it fell; and the ruin of that house was great.
> —LUKE 6:46–49

How is our foundation being built? Is it built on doing, going, and being as we have been instructed to do, or as we like to build it? Is it our values or God's? Everyone one of us needs to look in the mirror and ask ourselves how many angels rejoiced because of our works? Do we please people or God? Most of the time, we will find we are more pleased with ourselves than God is pleased with us!

Read the book of Acts and understand that it is about the activities of the apostles and the birthing of the church. We need to read this book to look for the important and paramount criteria of what we deem "church." We all know the great works of the original apostles. Yet there is not one recorded fund-raiser for a new donkey or camel! There is not one mention of singing, sound systems, cafeterias, or bingo and carnival day. We have designed services to entertain ourselves, falsely portraying the real priority of our Lord, and have wrapped it up as pleasing and appropriate to God. We have been sold this package, completely missing what really pleases God.

There is absolutely nothing wrong with singing, it even scriptural to do so:

> For both he that sanctifieth and they who are sanctified are all of one: for which cause he is not ashamed to call them brethren, Saying, I will declare thy name unto my brethren, in the midst of the church will I sing praise unto thee.
> —HEBREWS 2:11–12

It is wrong, however, when it becomes the focus and is made more important than the Word of God. Just look at the church service: how much time is spent on the Word and the message compared to all other activity? Then we have the well-trained preacher who has installed a clock on the back wall to make sure people are not detained by hearing a message that may help us grow. Consider this: have you ever seen a timer for the choir? So, why the pastor? Because the choir is entertainment and that is what we really came for.

> But the hour cometh, and now is, when the true worshippers shall worship the Father in spirit and in truth: for the Father seeketh such to worship him. God is a Spirit: and they that worship him must worship him in spirit and in truth.
> —JOHN 4:23–24

In truth! Do we spend more on electricity than missions? In truth, is our comfort more important than some old soul in some part of town or the world we have never heard of? In truth, is more time spent working on the music, new songs, and practices than reaching the lost? What is the priority of our church as well as ourselves? We will be judged on what we have done personally and our rewards in heaven will be based on our accomplishments for the Lord. So, our works for the Lord will always be about us, as individuals as well. How much time is spent on programs to make our services more entertaining for our benefit? Is more time spent on these things than on reaching the lost? If our church's efforts of time, money, and energy are being spent on non-fruit-producing activities, we may need to give thought to this verse:

> For where two or three are gathered together in my name, there am I in the midst of them.
>
> —MATTHEW 18:20

We know the Word of God is truth, therefore if we are gathered in His name Jesus is there. Can we stand in the very presence of Jesus in our churches and honestly state we are fulfilling His commandments? Do we have the right priority? Is it how Jesus would do it, or how we want it? Is it about us?

In truth, is it a fact that we have made it clear we want our pastor in our pulpit and accessible to us at all times and not out saving souls in some other country or even a different town? In truth, have we made it clear that we pay the bills, and the pastor doesn't need to be out trying to save a bunch of lost people that we don't even know. If they want to be saved, let them come to our church. They will be welcomed there, right? Sure, just as long as they don't sit in my seat. How many of us and our churches have wants and needs that outweigh the needs of the lost? It should be that way, we are the important ones, we are the church, and it should be about *me*. We think this is a very isolated condition, but it's not. It is more the norm. The church is failing and this is one of the main reasons.

There are many churches that are so busy praising and worshiping their God that they do not have time to serve Him. There was the best of the best worshipper ever created by God for that very purpose not so long ago. I do not believe we can even start to imagine what he sounded like, but it must have been wonderfully great. His name was Lucifer, the fallen star. Now we simply call him the devil. Let us make sure we are not doing his work by being like he was.

And why call ye me, Lord, Lord, and do not the things which
I say? Whosoever cometh to me, and heareth my sayings, and
doeth them, I will shew you to whom he is like: He is like a man
which built an house, and digged deep, and laid the foundation
on a rock: and when the flood arose, the stream beat vehemently
upon that house, and could not shake it: for it was founded upon
a rock. But he that heareth, and doeth not, is like a man that without a foundation built an house upon the earth; against which the
stream did beat vehemently, and immediately it fell; and the ruin
of that house was great.

—LUKE 6:46–49

In truth, do we put our wants and needs, our satisfaction, our
church activity, and our individual spiritual feeding by our pastor
first? In almost every church the answer is *yes.* If you go to a church
when the pastor is away, and the congregation is there, seeking God,
working for the body, and encouraging the person speaking, you'll be
in a spiritually sound and well-fed church. That church has a great
pastor, with outstanding teaching. The normal way for most pastors
to be gone is by not letting the congregation know that they will be
gone so that everyone will show up. In well-pastored churches that
have been spiritually grown, letting the congregation know the pastor
is going to be away will rally the people to support the speaker. These
are the congregations who are happy to share their pastors and do, in
fact, send them out as much as possible to help others. They are congregations of mature, grown Christians. They have a good pastor and
have learned well. They come to seek God and not some person, even
if it is their pastor. They know to put their pastor in his place, and that
place is always behind God. These congregations are servants of God,
serving through a pastor. There is a lot being said about cloning these
days—these churches are the ones that need to be cloned.

Do you want your church to be blessed by God? Do you want to be
blessed by God? Then turn off the air-conditioning sweat a little, and
spend the money on missions. Tell the pastor you are going to help
him grow and go, grow to what God intended. Send him to the lost,
tell him if someone needs prayer in his absence, you understand that
it's He that is in him and is the same that is in you, and you'll pray for

119

the people until the pastor returns. In fact, you should say, "Pastor, make sure I pray for you before you leave."

Pastors must help the people understand it is Jesus, not the pastor. The day it becomes about the pastor is the day the church starts to die. Pastors, feed your flock the real Word of God. Grow your people from milk to meat. You know you're responsible for them, and you will answer to God for them. But please, for their sakes, for your sake, and the sake of the kingdom of God, make sure your church and your flock understands this important fact.

You are God's servant, chosen to serve His people. However, you can only serve them by being God's servant, first and foremost. Make sure you and they know who you work for. You may be paid by the church, but your employment is with God!

> No servant can serve two masters: for either he will hate the one, and love the other; or else he will hold to the one, and despise the other. Ye cannot serve God and mammon.
> —Luke 16:13

Pastors, explain to your people that you trust in God, you were called by God, and will be provided for by God. The day you start trusting in and following some board for your needs and directions, you have stopped working for your God. Pastors, this is important: God is a jealous God, and is to have no other gods before Him. Who is your God? Be very very clear here, your ministry and maybe your soul is at stake. Man and Satan have worked hard to add requirements, creeds, and deeds to you. Shake them off. Tell them that in the name of Jesus, you rebuke that worldly stuff. Tell them that, of course, they can hold you to a higher standard; yes, we will work together; and yes, you understand your position with the church. However, what is important for us all to know is your position. Tell your congregation that you serve God and they serve you. If they do not get that, they do not get you. If this is not your pastor, start with the dung, keep up the digging, and begin pruning.

These are the men and women of God that are pastors who are fulfilling a calling from God, and are doing it God's way. If you do not have one get one, grow one, and soon!

He that is not with me is against me; and he that gathereth not
with me scattereth abroad.

—MATTHEW 12:30

Know this: if you're not serving your Lord, you are serving Satan.
Satan can be and is often packaged as a bunch of well-meaning church
members, just wanting what they think they deserve and need. Many
simply do not know better. It is not only the pastor's job to tell them,
it is your job, my job, and the job of every grown Christian. It is past
time that we all started to do our job. Anytime, and I mean anytime,
it's about the members, the board, or even the pastor, and not about
Jesus, you're not serving God. Worldly things are Satan's things. He is
a great deceiver who has and is deceiving many well-meaning souls to
join his kingdom.

Many have died to hell's domain getting what they wanted from a
failing pastor, instead of what they needed from a man or woman of
God. You might want to read that statement over again; it is the truth!
Many are now in churches that have a minister of Satan as a pastor,
and they will burn in hell. Are they getting what they deserve? No,
they deserve what Jesus has already purchased for them. They deserve
to have us that know the truth, to stand and be what is needed in
the kingdom of God. They deserve to have Christians and churches
that love them more than they love themselves. They deserve to have
pastors that were literally birthed in Christ, raised in His light, and
matured as trees that will always stand and forever more be great trees
of endurance!

Chapter Six

TREES OF MAGNITUDE

How many different types of fruit can one expect to grow on a single tree? In fact, how many limbs can one tree have? How much diversity can we expect our pastors to have grown in proficiently? What should we expect from these men and women of God in all the areas of ministries? We, as individuals, evaluate the church, the service, the building, and all other activities differently. From our own experience and needs we all have what we perceive as their importance. There are cultural differences, age differences, and simply our personal preferences. We all are different with different tastes. The church tries to meet as many of these preferences as possible. There is no right or wrong except in matters of always being spiritually correct. They are just differences, and we need to be considerate and accommodating to all.

Unfortunately, however, there are many people today that want their church to meet them in their moral condition and worldly preferences. They think the church should move to where and what society has declared as right. They have what are considered conditions and superior educational knowledge that rate high above the Bible and God. These are people who believe that there is a far better new and modern way to be spiritual and that they have found it.

According to many, the old and outdated ideas in the Bible no longer apply. This mentality is sweeping across denominational lines and entering into our seminaries. This is wrong and we, as a body of Christ, need to be standing up and declaring it for what it is, which is worldly and sinful. We need great and bold pastors speaking out and proclaiming the truth. The truth is that many seemingly successful churches are nothing but a gathering of hell-bound, "tickle my ears," spiritually lost souls. God wants them to be saved as much as He does you and I. In order to rise to this challenge we must not quit and we must set in place uncompromising pastors, pastors of magnitude! There is a mighty need to grow these kind of pastors. As a general rule, they have not been grown lately. I have called these desirable pastors "trees of magnitude." One of the definitions of *magnitude* is, according to *Webster's Dictionary*, is that of "the brightness of a celestial body on a logarithmic scale" How appropriate magnitude is for these men and women of God.

In our quest to reach these precious and lost souls we must be open-minded. Many times the more traditional churches fail to compare or compete with these churches. Remember, we are a business and we have competition, and it is Satan. We need churches that are equally successful, equally exciting, and meeting the people's needs, but with God's Word!

Pastors need to teach that sometimes being a Christian is not easy, sometimes we just can't do what we used to. We can't even think the same thoughts we used to. There is a covenant that must be honored and obeyed. We will be judged and we all need the correct teaching to be prepared to meet our Lord. We need churches with pastors capable of meeting many needs to reach many people. The fact is, pastors can't do this—not alone. Let me say this again: pastors can't do this—not alone. They cannot be all things to all people. They cannot be expected to do every part of the ministry well. They do need to be able to oversee all aspects and especially the spiritual teaching.

This job becomes much easier with a Word-filled church. We hear a lot about Spirit-filled churches, and that is really great. But I truly believe we have lost our focus by not allowing our churches to compete and meet their real objective—souls! We need the power of the

Holy Ghost working in our churches. We have failed by believing that power is in demonstrations and shows that are for our entertainment. The result is a lot of activity and excitement but no change in the church, neither are we adding to the kingdom. We are then the mighty power of God doing nothing except entertaining ourselves, offering nothing of consequence to the lost and dying world. What is needed is the Word of God to be taught correctly and understood in a congregation with the power of God's spirit. That kind of church will win back the neighborhoods and the nations.

We must grow pastors that are capable of managing, as well as establishing, the needs and priorities of their congregations. It must be God's plan, not man's, and not our way. This growth is hard for pastors, and few grow healthy and strong in this area. Failure to produce fruit abundantly and continually is often a result of this growth period. It is one of the most complex, hardest-to-get-right periods of growth. We fail to grow healthy and hardy pastors because everyone has a different expectation and plan. Then the growing pastor is trying to meet all these expectations and directions from so many people. The result is they simply grow in too many ways and do not become strong in any. They end up growing poorly, unfocused, unorganized, and are simply made up of many branches, but are certainly not a tree. If there is no clear direction with defined, achievable goals, these pastors will always fail.

> Where there is no vision, the people perish: but he that keepeth the law, happy is he.
>
> —PROVERBS 29:18

We need to understand the problems that can result during this process and be aware of how to recognize these destroying demons in the future. Failure here can result in no fruit. It can also result in a lot of fruit, but most every apple on the tree has worms in it and spoils before becoming ripe. This period can be at almost anytime in a pastor's life but comes most often after a period of church growth. If we really look honestly at the conditions of our churches and nation, we will visibly see what kind of pastors the world has been growing. As I have tried to stress, we just need to keep looking at the fruit.

The wonderful men and women of God, who are answering God's call and allowing God to work through them, need to examine themselves. What are their greatest talents, where do they need to manage hands on, and where do they just need to allow others to implement under their spiritual oversight? Let me again state that one of the main problems is that most of the churches have failed to recognize and accept that the pastor is the boss. We need pastors under the head of the church, Jesus Christ, and the church needs to be under them. For most of us, this is harder than giving up our seat to a visitor at our church.

A few areas that need to be managed are music and the choir, children's programs and Bible studies, teen programs and Bible studies, adult programs and Bible studies, outreach programs and missionaries, evangelism of local, national, and international fields, the nursery, ushers and greeters, the sound system, not to mention seating and the thermostat. I do not believe any pastor yet has achieved the anointing to set a thermostat to please everyone. Some are hot and some cold, and somebody had to make a decision as to who it is that is going to be uncomfortable. Few decisions will please everyone, but they must be made nevertheless.

Making decisions is a real problem every pastor must overcome, and they need our help badly. God has given them a special heart, loving and caring and full of compassion. It is very hard for them to disappoint anyone. They really can't stand hurting anyone's feelings. When we spiritual dwarfs do not get the decisions we want, we get our feelings hurt. Many pastors in our churches end up not making decisions at an appropriate time just to avoid this.

The fear of making decisions, especially in pastors, will cripple a church. There are many departments and staff members in our churches, mostly volunteer, that will never produce much if anything, yet they remain. Often, this is simply because the pastor will not make a decision because he is afraid of hurting someone's feelings. These churches will reach a minimal growth level and become stagnant. They will never grow past the capabilities in place. There is improper management in all departments, including ushering, greeters, teachers, and associate pastors that is never corrected. Pastors pray for growth they can't manage and that never comes. If the church were managed as a business, with great concern for the lost souls not being reached, the needed changes would be ordered and adhered to. One of the first places a church should send their pastor is to a business management course. Every decision not made in a timely manner only gets worse. Problems only get bigger.

Here is where pastors must see past people's feelings and be able to make decisions that get the needed results and not just a desired outcome. These decisions can affect the nations. We can all help the pastors make decisions by taking our feelings out of the process.

The easiest decisions to be made are those involved around spiritual things. These can and should always be made according to God's Word. Here God gave us set instructions that are easy to understand and the same for all. People have to accept it when it's a God thing.

The other decisions are the ones people get mad over and allow their feelings to be hurt because the outcome didn't please them. Each of these decisions will be received and perceived differently by most people. The new mother who goes to drop off her newborn at the nursery will be using her nose and eyes most observantly. If she finds a problem here, then she is gone. She may decide the whole church is not right because the person over the nursery failed to see the importance of cleanliness. The nursery volunteer may have many children of her own and is not as concerned as she was with her first. Or, perhaps there is a shortage of volunteers (as there usually is in churches), and the nursery volunteer actually handles several other jobs in addition to handling the nursery. Is either woman wrong? No. They just have different priorities and needs and are at different places in experience. Regardless, the church failed because the nursery failed, and this is because of the fact that only 8 percent of the people in the church are helping. Things weren't clean because there was just no one to help. Do we think we will not be held accountable if, because of this scenario (or any other similar experience), this mother never goes to a church again and she and her whole family are lost to an eternal hell? This is an answer the other 92 percent who do nothing better find out about.

Your pastor may really be in to singing and studying music. He may have been a music pastor before at a large church. If so, it's likely that the church programs will involve a lot of music. If you personally do not care that much for music and want to hear the Word of God more than music, who's wrong? Neither. The larger the church, the more different opinions there are. These differences can and often do cause ill feelings, hurt feelings, and often anger.

Anything that causes division is of Satan and cannot be allowed to remain in the church. Let me make sure we all get this: if it causes division, it is of *Satan!* The problem is us. If we were all grown in Christ enough to not allow these problems to distract us from Jesus, we wouldn't need a pastor to start with. We must understand our problems and personal shortcomings and not let them become part of the church's and pastor's problems. We must also understand that God has decided to use men and women for pastors, and people are not perfect. They are chosen, anointed, and led by God, but they are still mere humans. The very best will be just like us. They will get it wrong once in a while. The fact is, maybe God should have stuck with the donkey, like in the Book of Numbers, the twenty-second chapter. The donkey got it right every time, which is a much better record than any of us have, and that for sure includes pastors.

We must get real, keep going, and be in unity. We need to get behind our pastors even when they make mistakes, no matter what. In fact, there may be times that some of us need to get in front of him to prevent the mistake in the first place. Sometimes we need to be in front to take the blows and heat that can hurt the pastor. There is a strong possibility the mistake happened because the pastor was so busy and burdened trying to help someone as helpless as most of us really are. Forgive, forget, and forge on in unity. I have seen what happens to a great church and great pastor when unity is not a priority. A church without unity in the body will fail.

> Behold, how good and how pleasant it is for brethren to dwell together in unity! It is like the precious ointment upon the head, that ran down upon the beard, even Aaron's beard: that went down to the skirts of his garments; as the dew of Hermon, and as the dew that descended upon the mountains of Zion: for there the LORD commanded the blessing, even life for evermore.
>
> —PSALM 133

I changed the seating one morning in our church, using the same chairs with the same service. I changed nothing but where the people sat. Many people were very upset. They wanted to sit where they always sat. Is it wrong to sit in the same seats all the time? No! However, when where we sit is more important than serving God and offering up praise and thanksgiving, it's wrong. If the seating arrangement is more important than our focus on Jesus and the service, we really need to spend time in the Word of God and grow ourselves. After all, our church is supposed to be a house of prayer, not a house of comfort!

These areas I have mentioned are not nearly inclusive as potential problems. There are countless others. It is only important that we learn how to prevent and get past these differences and not blame. I truly have the answer that will help every person involved in any program know when the problem is theirs, or in fact is someone else's. If it is about you, it's wrong. If someone is trying to get something their way so it's about them, it's wrong. It's wrong every time it's not about Jesus. In real short terms, it is almost always about us and we are usually wrong. Here is an important question and one that should open our eyes. Where would our churches be if we spent as much time trying to get it God's way as we do trying to get it our way? Where would we each be individually if we spent as much time looking for our faults as we do in finding and seeing them in others? If we are going to call ourselves Christians, visible to the world, we must see the truth in these two questions.

We also must grow personally and corporately. Until we do, most of the body of Christ would do better by keeping their mouths closed except during prayer and praise and worship. It is important to know that we can be used by Satan to hurt and destroy our brothers and sisters, as well as our pastors. We end up working against God!

We must realize how many different programs a pastor is forced to try to do just because we can't get along and won't do it someone else's way. Most of us have a real problem submitting to authority, especially when it's that person who just rubs us the wrong way. How on God's green earth has that person been put in that place of authority over that department? Surely it's of Satan. No! More than likely it was our fault because we failed to grow and we couldn't be in obedience, so the pastor could not use us. It should be about Jesus, and we all need to really understand what He said about being a servant.

> And whosoever will be chief among you, let him be your servant: Even as the Son of man came not to be ministered unto, but to minister, and to give his life a ransom for many.
> —MATTHEW 20:27–28

When we understand and grow to the point of really being useful to God, all of us mighty men and women of God will be assisting the ushers and others in the "helps" department. There we will find some people who have been serving people and God for a long time. They have gotten it right, and we need to learn from them. We also need to be real friendly to these people, remembering their birthdays and a gift at Christmas in hopes that in heaven they will let us visit them in their rewards. They will be uptown in the best mansions that have been reserved for the real servants of God. If there are alleys of gold, there are many of us that will have a garage apartment on them and our rewards will be few.

We must learn this: if we have not been a good servant to our pastor, as well to others, we'll never be good in any position of authority. We are not useable to our pastor or to God. God will not allow us to be moved up to a position of authority. We must submit to Jesus; submit to those placed over us including that one person who somehow got put in charge of the thing you felt was yours to do. Remember David and wait upon the Lord and stop griping, gossiping, and complaining. Start helping and praying. If we are not ready to set an example spiritually, we can't set a good example physically. Many of us would make an outstanding servant if we could just use our tongue and be able to tell others. If we are one of those who uses our tongue more than our hands and back, we are not serving, we are telling. We are not helping, but we are in fact hindering.

It's hard to submit to someone, and even more so when they appear to be less capable. But it's never about us or our abilities. It can never be about a pastor or his abilities either. It must always be about Jesus and what He does in and through us. This is why many times that incapable, unskilled and not very smart person we know of has ministry works that always succeed. They were smart enough to know they could not do it, but Jesus in them could. All of us really smart and capable characters keep trying to do it by our great abilities and keep failing.

So, how do we grow a pastor of magnitude during this process? First, we must understand the areas that the pastors are the strongest in, and those they are gifted in. At this point, we will find he's not like the one we used to have and he's not like the one on television that we like so well. He is not going to be like any other pastor. We must understand this and learn to appreciate the uniqueness of the pastor that God sent us. If we have sought God and fasted and prayed before selecting a pastor, we must realize that they are there by divine appointment. The church has failed because we have been choosing pastors that fulfill what we want and how we want it. That is the reason this country is in the state of moral degradation that it is. It's time to change directions and go toward God, not man. God will not change to our wants and desires. In truth, born-again Christians are to be growing in what God wants and how they can be useful to Him. How often do we think about what we can do for God, instead of praying for God to do something for us?

All pastors should be acting like Jesus' and they are just going to act differently. Look at the apostles, how very different they were, yet how they were alike when it came to God's Word and the spreading of the gospel of Jesus Christ. Their words, lives, suffering, and deaths were all different, but still similar. Everything was always about Jesus and the kingdom of God.

Pastors and Christians must grab on to this fact: if we are to fulfill God's calling on our lives and our churches, pastors as well as congregations will always be different. If we truly trust in God, we will be able to appreciate and accept why God sent this pastor to this congregation. Many times and in many churches pastors just do not work out. Why? Because God keeps sending us what we need and not what we want. We must grow up and grow past our wants.

> Then said Jesus unto his disciples, If any man will come after me, let him deny himself, and take up his cross, and follow me. For

whosoever will save his life shall lose it: and whosoever will lose his life for my sake shall find it. For what is a man profited, if he shall gain the whole world, and lose his own soul? or what shall a man give in exchange for his soul? For the Son of man shall come in the glory of his Father with his angels; and then he shall reward every man according to his works. Verily I say unto you, There be some standing here, which shall not taste of death, till they see the Son of man coming in his kingdom.

—MATTHEW 16:24–28

Every aspect of serving God must start with our own sinful, human death. We must die to ourselves, to our wants and desires, and even to our own beliefs. We must let God be God of our life. One of the hardest things that we preach and teach, but seldom really grasp, is that we serve a risen Christ; He is not dead and not asleep, but seated at the right hand of the Father. He is active in our lives, but only when we let Him, and only in His time. We do not let, neither do we wait, but we do! Unfortunately, when we do, many times we do so without Jesus. The church and this nation have failed because the church does not believe in this simple principal: God will do what He said He will do!

This witness is true. Wherefore rebuke them sharply, that they may be sound in the faith; Not giving heed to Jewish fables, and commandments of men, that turn from the truth. Unto the pure all things are pure: but unto them that are defiled and unbelieving is nothing pure; but even their mind and conscience is defiled. They profess that they know God; but in works they deny him, being abominable, and disobedient, and unto every good work reprobate.

—TITUS 1:13–16

How many of us are guilty of this? In many churches, as well as our personal lives, we confess Jesus, but our works deny Him. Our lives do not reflect Him, and no one can tell we are a son or daughter of God. To grow a pastor of magnitude, we must see that our works do not deny Jesus. This sounds so simple, why should we waste paper and ink putting it in writing? It is, quite simply, the biggest problem and lack in almost every pastor and church; every church, not only in the United

States, but also the world. The vast majority of the fruit in this nation and the world is not the fruit of Christ. We must always, always look at the fruit. Let's all help and allow our pastors to grow by avoiding this pitfall from hell. Let's also regrow every pastor that for whatever reason missed the mark, regardless of his age or position. Regrow, do not throw out, do not ship out, but help make a fruit-producing pastor. We could all find faults. We can and normally do point the finger the other way. Let's grow up and just join our hands and hearts and get to work.

I have a lot of godly respect for every pastor. I would like to point out here that the following words are spoken in love. They are spoken from my love of Jesus and His church, my brothers and sisters in Christ. Above all, however, they are spoken for my love for the lost.

You wimpy, weak-kneed pastors speak to tickle your congregation's ears instead of boldly speaking God's Word by growing and leading those that you have under your charge to fulfill God's plan. Repent, get help, and start over. You're doing more for Satan than you are for God, and you know it. You are afraid to take a stand because you are afraid you may be fired. Decide now for whom you want to work. The people or God? If you are called a servant of God, then start serving Him. Pastors, the day you think the congregation to whom you minister is your security and your provision, instead of God being your provider, please get some counseling from other successful pastors. You must choose your Master. Whom is it that you really serve? Pastors, please, this is real: you have a Boss. Know who your Boss is!

Tell your church: here is the real Word of God and we have some really bad, and some really good news. The bad news is that many of you are going to burn in hell if you do not repent and get right with God! The good news is that it's not too late, and I am now going to be the pastor God called me to really be and I'll show you the way. Those of you that want things to be the same old way, there is the door. The pastor down the street is still on Satan's side, I suggest you go there, you'll fit right in.

That one paragraph, if taken to heart by our pastors and applied, would save the many millions already sitting in the church. That would be a real revival! It could be done in a matter of days, as Jesus would show up and help His church. We would be able to leave the natural and enter into the supernatural. If we have a supernatural Father, Son, and Holy Ghost, and God said He would dwell in us, why do we keep drudgingly working in the natural? We are sons and daughters of the supernatural God, let's start acting like it.

Now back to abilities and diversities. We need to get pastors in the right zone. When pastors have to micromanage hands-on, and not just oversee because Jack can't get along with Fred, something has to suffer. When pastors are required to work on programs that do not involve their strong abilities and gifts, at least two programs suffer. The one the pastor is not best qualified to do suffers and the one he is qualified for but doesn't have time to do is suffering. We need to get this right. There are many great pastors that are not getting their work done and not doing what God has called them to do because they are doing our work instead. It's our fault.

First, men and women of the church, please take Jack and Fred or Jane and Sally aside in love and explain what is really happening and what the result of their shortcomings are. Tell them it's not acceptable and that things are no longer going to be about them. Most of us never really realize what we are and what we have done. If the men and women of the church did this, the pastor would not have to handle it himself.

Pastors, please don't let yourselves get dragged down into trying to do all things at the cost of not doing the ones you were called to do well. Raise up people who understand the needs of the church and trust God to supply. How many times has God wanted to fill a gap but someone, who is not called for the position, was standing in the way? It could even be the pastor trying to do what someone else was called to do. Jesus is the best example and taught us how to be servants. He also sent and had all of His congregation going and doing. The apostles also did this early on in their ministry.

Shamefully, six thousand pastors leave the ministry monthly, and we wonder why. We are in the last days! We do not have any time to lose, and we desperately need every man and woman of God! We the church, the body of Christ, must understand we can't grow that which we have lost. We must be about growing pastors that can stand, and then stand. We also need to be getting some of these truly called pastors back in the churches, fully equipped and supported. In doing so, we also need to get the demons of hell out from behind the pulpits.

> Wherefore take unto you the whole armour of God, that ye may be able to withstand in the evil day, and having done all, to stand. Stand therefore, having your loins girt about with truth, and having on the breastplate of righteousness.
>
> —EPHESIANS 6:13–14

One of the big problems in many churches is having to skip around some of the Bible. If a church is not charismatic, it must review Corinthians with "this is for now," and "that was for times past and died out." Then we have the Charismatic church that accepts it is as now and wants to achieve all things by casting the demons out of it and by praying in tongues. This book is not trying to teach any particular faith but, like some others, I will not dodge the issue. We are about raising up pastors that are going to make a difference. Let's look at 1 Corinthians 12:

> Now concerning spiritual gifts, brethren, I would not have you ignorant. Ye know that ye were Gentiles, carried away unto these dumb idols, even as ye were led. Wherefore I give you to understand, that no man speaking by the Spirit of God calleth Jesus accursed: and that no man can say that Jesus is the Lord, but by the Holy Ghost. Now there are diversities of gifts, but the same Spirit. And there are differences of administrations, but the same Lord. And there are diversities of operations, but it is the same God which worketh all in all. But the manifestation of the Spirit is given to every man to profit withal. For to one is given by the Spirit the word of wisdom; to another the word of knowledge by the same Spirit; To another faith by the same Spirit; to another the gifts of healing by the same Spirit; To another the working of miracles; to another prophecy; to another discerning of spirits; to another divers kinds of tongues; to another the interpretation of tongues: But all these worketh that one and the selfsame Spirit, dividing to every man severally as he will. For as the body is one, and hath many members, and all the members of that one body, being many, are one body: so also is Christ. For by one Spirit are

we all baptized into one body, whether we be Jews or Gentiles, whether we be bond or free; and have been all made to drink into one Spirit. For the body is not one member, but many. If the foot shall say, Because I am not the hand, I am not of the body; is it therefore not of the body? And if the ear shall say, Because I am not the eye, I am not of the body; is it therefore not of the body? If the whole body were an eye, where were the hearing? If the whole were hearing, where were the smelling? But now hath God set the members every one of them in the body, as it hath pleased him. And if they were all one member, where were the body? But now are they many members, yet but one body. And the eye cannot say unto the hand, I have no need of thee: nor again the head to the feet, I have no need of you. Nay, much more those members of the body, which seem to be more feeble, are necessary: And those members of the body, which we think to be less honourable, upon these we bestow more abundant honour; and our uncomely parts have more abundant comeliness. For our comely parts have no need: but God hath tempered the body together, having given more abundant honour to that part which lacked: That there should be no schism in the body; but that the members should have the same care one for another. And whether one member suffer, all the members suffer with it; or one member be honoured, all the members rejoice with it. Now ye are the body of Christ, and members in particular. And God hath set some in the church, first apostles, secondarily prophets, thirdly teachers, after that miracles, then gifts of healings, helps, governments, diversities of tongues. Are all apostles? are all prophets? are all teachers? are all workers of miracles? Have all the gifts of healing? do all speak with tongues? do all interpret? But covet earnestly the best gifts: and yet shew I unto you a more excellent way.

—1 CORINTHIANS 12

If we are going to grow pastors of magnitude to change the world, we must have our churches in unity. Let us look at this very important Word of God. It's time that we look at our differences in an honest and constructive manner. If you are a member of a denomination that does not believe in the gifts, I'm not here to persuade you otherwise. In fact, I believe that every denomination that is blood-bought is a part of the body. Furthermore, I believe God's Word is very clear. We need to be more about getting ourselves and our churches right and in the will of God rather than worrying about what's wrong in some other church. It's not wrong, it's just different. Many times we look at these verses and think only of the different people in our local church body. I'm quite sure, however, that God will put together a bride for His Son and it will be perfectly fit and not divisive. God's Word says, "one church without spot or wrinkle." We must, in these days, ask ourselves, do we really think that our particular church is the only one that is right? It's time to be God's sons and daughters, from the driest fundamentalist to the hoop-hollering Pentecostal. We need to get together. One is going to be a foot, and another a leg so let's start walking together now for our Lord and the souls we can jointly save.

Let's look at 1 Corinthians 12 a little more closely. Verse 1 states, "I would not have you ignorant." Yet many of us are. We are completely ignorant when we refuse to work with someone who may be baptized in the Holy Ghost and walking in the gifts. When we ourselves are baptized in the name of the Father, Son, and Holy Ghost, He dwells in us. The same Spirit dwells in us all in unity and not in division. Division is of Satan.

If we know there is only one God, Son, and Holy Ghost and we refuse to work with or help, and even reject the congregation down the street, can we grasp who we rejected? We rejected God, and this puts us in the same company as the Pharisees and Sadducees.

Verses 4 and 5: "diversities of gifts" and "differences of administrations." We the church have differences, and our pastor has differences. In fact, all pastors and churches have diversities and they all are not capable of doing all things equally well. Time spent struggling with works that were meant for someone else to do takes away from the works they were called to do. Church, we need to raise our pastors up from doing all things and let them flow into their gifted areas.

Verses 7–10: these verses talk about the nine gifts of the Holy Ghost. There are many who have stood dogmatically against the mention of these. They believe they were true for a period of time and now have died out. I'm comfortable leaving these alone in this book, except in the area where we are looking at growing our pastors and unity in our churches. Your pastor has gifts. We can call them gifts of the Holy Ghost, inherited traits, learned abilities, or anything we want. The important thing here is that the gifts are used to the betterment of the pastor and the whole body of Christ. Every church, and I really do mean every church—even those who are not charismatic, really expect their pastor to be able to pray into being seven of the nine gifts. We just look at it differently, and that's okay. If we are sick, we want the pastor to pray for healing. If we need something that is just plain impossible in the natural, we want a miracle. We hope our pastor has knowledge and that his understanding is from God. We want our pastors to know what is going to happen so we can be prepared. What church wants a pastor without faith? We hope our pastor discerns the times. Every Bible-believing church agrees on these, just in different ways. Are they a spirit? Are they a gift? Let's just agree they are from God and are to be used to benefit the church.

Okay, so what do we do with the other two—tongues and interpretation of tongues? It's simple! Do what you feel is right, and understand that, in reality, we agree on seven out of nine, or 78 percent. The fact is, we don't agree with 78 percent of the people in our own church, yet we let it divide us and our pastor's capability to work with others in the community. My God, our pastors might catch something from those Pentecostals, or one of them will cast out something. We all need to get real and grow in Christ. The real and extremely sad fact is that many churches in this country have spent more time worrying about how other churches are doing it wrong than worrying about Satan. Satan is very well-pleased with an awful lot of churches, and that is a fact that must change

Verse 12: the body is one, all the members are one, "so also is Christ." We are one, saved by the same blood, adopted to Abraham, one tribe, one God, one Christ, one salvation, one heaven, one, one, and one! Church and pastors, anytime either a church, pastor, or individual tries to make the body of Christ anything but one body, it is wrong and it is of Satan!

Verse 18: God set the members, every one, "as it hath pleased Him." When we don't understand the church down the street and don't want our pastor or our church to mess with that bunch, we are out of God's will. Remember this, God put them there and it pleased Him. How can we not want to work together with that which pleased God? It's simple, when it's about us and only our way, we are ignorant, as verse one points out.

Verse 25: "There should be no schism in the body." That means no division. Please be careful; Satan is the great deceiver. Let's grow pastors to work with all followers of Jesus. Let's learn from our differences, and gain corporately from our strengths.

I have tried to stress this should be a business, the Father's business. I also have tried desperately to point out we have allowed our competitor to succeed in our place. The church must become unified! Please think about this. What if all the McDonald's franchises started cooking hamburgers all differently, or started serving other kinds of foods altogether. Instead of being successful and in unity, they would fail and be divided and separate. They would just be like all the other mom-and-pop sandwich places. That is what has happened to the churches. We are not a unified force against morality, and we have little or no political clout. The church is just a bunch of separate little storefronts not making a significant difference anywhere. Why can't the churches reach across those man-made divisions and denominations by joining forces in a unified approach? We could change this country in a matter of a few weeks back to one nation under God, by God, and for God's purpose.

Verses 27–31: "Ye are the body of Christ…God hath set some in the church," as well as the gifts. But we see in chapter 13 that the most important commandment of all is *charity*. I know that many will receive this negatively. Change comes hard for most of us. Can we visualize ourselves or our churches in the following context? Can we imagine a conversation between the eye and ear? The eye tells the ear, "You should be seeing. Because you are not seeing, you have missed all the great things God has made." The ear then tells the eye, "You need to stop looking and start listening, and then you could hear all the praise being given to God and all the wonderful sounds." Now I ask you, who is right? Neither or both? In our little way of looking and knowing, our ways are not God's ways. How do we let this divide? If we believe that the Bible is the inspired Word of God, we must also believe God does not change.

139

Unity and agreement in the body of Christ is not an option, it is a commandment. Please remember these words for they are God's.

> Behold, how good and how pleasant it is for brethren to dwell together in unity! It is like the precious ointment upon the head, that ran down upon the beard, even Aaron's beard: that went down to the skirts of his garments; As the dew of Hermon, and as the dew that descended upon the mountains of Zion: for there the LORD commanded the blessing, even life for evermore.
>
> —PSALM 133

Let us be family, sons and daughters, brothers and sisters that are in agreement. Only then can the lost start taking us more seriously. How would Jesus want us to be? Would Jesus love the people that are doing it wrong in the church down the street? Do the people down the street love Jesus? Jesus spoke of the importance of love, often using the word *charity,* in the Bible. Are these words an example of our lives and our churches?

> Now the end of the commandment is charity out of a pure heart, and of a good conscience, and of faith unfeigned.
>
> —1 TIMOTHY 1:5

> Let no man despise thy youth; but be thou an example of the believers, in word, in conversation, in charity, in spirit, in faith, in purity. Till I come, give attendance to reading, to exhortation, to doctrine. Neglect not the gift that is in thee, which was given thee by prophecy, with the laying on of the hands of the presbytery. Meditate upon these things; give thyself wholly to them; that thy profiting may appear to all. Take heed unto thyself, and unto the doctrine; continue in them: for in doing this thou shalt both save thyself, and them that hear thee.
>
> —1 TIMOTHY 4:12–16

> And though I have the gift of prophecy, and understand all mysteries, and all knowledge; and though I have all faith, so that I could remove mountains, and have not charity, I am nothing.
>
> —1 CORINTHIANS 13:2

The Word of God clearly states how we win the lost!

> For in doing this thou shalt both save thyself, and them that hear thee.

> —1 TIMOTHY 4:16

Are we really concerned with the lost or are we caught up in how we think God's church should be like *we* think it should be? It's as if we think God cannot take care of His own church. I am sure the bride of Christ will be just what Jesus said it would be, without spot or wrinkle.

Chapter Seven

PERPETUAL GROWTH

In the previous chapters, we have discussed the pitfalls or hindrances that not only destroy us personally, but also the body of Christ. Many of these are because of our human nature, which is not godly. Many more are because Satan is active in our churches. Today, so many churches and Christians are similar to Christmas. There is a lot of noise and activity enhanced by an extreme amount of excitement with very little said about Jesus. Where is the birth of Christ seen in our Christmas traditions? It's disheartening that most large retail chains will no longer allow their cashiers to say "Merry Christmas" because it may offend someone. Everyone who reads this book has purchased something from one of these places. Did we consider that God was offended when "Merry Christmas" was replaced by "Happy Holidays"? The day that was designated to celebrate the time when God came from heaven to earth for man now glorifies Satan more than God. You and I are a part of the problem. We allowed it, and we participate in it. It is not a happy holiday, it is a joyous day for those who know the Lord, and we should be telling cashiers. We need to let the stores know if it isn't about Jesus, if it is not "Merry Christmas," we will do our purchasing where it is acknowledged. We need the pastors who are willing to stand and be heard. We have allowed prayer to be removed, the Ten Commandments to be removed, and we have also allowed Christ to be removed from Christmas.

We must understand that many of us have grown up in this atmosphere, and it has become normal to us. It is not any one denomination's fault, or any one person or group in particular. It is something that Satan has stolen, little by little. The important thing here is not when or who was at fault when it happened. The understanding we must have is that Satan is responsible for it. It's important for us to realize that it's been done. We can no longer continue in some blind stupor and pretend that all is well. Satan has stolen Christmas as he has stolen many churches, allowing souls to stumble and fall into hell.

We have the power to take back everything Satan has stolen. All that is needed is people who know what is missing and understand the power God has given us. We must realize what we are up against in our churches and understand the job our pastors have in front of them. We need mighty warring pastors, men and women who are willing to step out and up to the frontlines where the battle is. Pastors who are hiding inside the four walls of a church and ignore there is a war going on will be of no help to God in these last days. Congregations must understand this and be willing to send their pastors out completely equipped for the job and covered in prayer. Elders and deacons need to read and study what an armor bearer is to God's chosen, and some of them need to become one.

The sad fact is that most churches and Christians really do not understand the presence and power of Satan. It is my prayer that after reading this book, they will see how much Jesus told us about Satan and his ways. We have failed, and failed miserably, in every area we were warned about. We call ourselves Christians, yet have not heeded His words and His instructions. I have mentioned this a lot, and wrote a lot about this subject, in great hopes we the body of Christ would grasp there is an active Satan.

> For we wrestle not against flesh and blood, but against principalities, against powers, against the rulers of the darkness of this world, against spiritual wickedness in high places.
> —Ephesians 6:12

There are some big problems that need to be fixed in the body of Christ, especially in our denominational churches. One of the biggest and hardest tasks ahead is for the churches to realize there is a problem. Here is where the churches need to look towards the businessmen and women in their churches. The successful businesspeople will know how to find the problems and formulate ideas on how to overcome them. Every successful business has plans and goals that lead to a result. In a business, a sale or product is made and a financial profit is the end result. There will be many different parts to the business operation, but all lead to and enhance the possibility of success at the end. All aspects are reviewed and continually monitored by looking for problems. Problems with products or personnel are immediately dealt with, sometimes in dismissal. It's always about the end result, with continued improvement to be better than a competitor.

Here lies the first obstacle in our churches that must be recognized and overcome. *Yes*, we have a competitor who is very experienced, most capable, and has had a much better success rate than the churches ever could hope for. We need to understand this, church; Satan is going to defeat us in every aspect if we do not understand this and know how to defeat him.

> Therefore hell hath enlarged herself, and opened her mouth without measure: and their glory, and their multitude, and their pomp, and he that rejoiceth, shall descend into it.
>
> —Isaiah 5:14

> Enter ye in at the strait gate: for wide is the gate, and broad is the way, that leadeth to destruction, and many there be which go in thereat: Because strait is the gate, and narrow is the way, which leadeth unto life, and few there be that find it.
>
> —Matthew 7:13–14

> The wicked shall be turned into hell, and all the nations that forget God. For the needy shall not always be forgotten: the expectation of the poor shall not perish for ever.
>
> —Psalm 9:17–18

How many of us have sat in a church year after year being fed by some pastor, yet never understanding that we are at war with Satan. Somewhere along the way many of us came to a false conclusion. Being born again does not make us overcomers. What it does is give us the authority and power in Jesus' name to overcome. We must run the race, and we must finish the race. Every step of the way, Satan is there to defeat us.

We are to be about our heavenly Father's business, and Satan is our competition. Souls are our business, our product. The great failure of our churches today is the failure to understand they are to be businesses. Their business is souls. Their goal is to save everyone. Their competition is Satan. God told us to save souls and Satan wants to keep them. The problem is that Satan is getting many more than we are. The Father's business, left in our hands, is failing to compete. The churches are happy with very little market share. There is no accountability in churches based on the business of souls. Success is measured in congregation size and monetary offerings. What appears to us as an extremely successful church many times is a failure, completely bankrupt in the Father's business. The fact is that in order to increase the market share it takes work, and the churches as a whole are not willing to work for that result. Many will work for some play to be put on. Others will volunteer for the musicals, dinners, and even the workday at the church. If we look at ourselves honestly, we see that we do the things that are entertaining to us; things about our building, our classes, but not much about others, which includes the lost! They also should be our business.

There is a great mind-set missing in our churches, and to get it back we need great pastors that will do more than preach. We need our pastors to lead. We must ask ourselves a very difficult question: are we the church stupid or just plain lazy? The fact is, these are the only two possible answers. We need to read the following verse with great care and seek understanding.

> Behold, I give unto you power to tread on serpents and scorpions, and over all the power of the enemy: and nothing shall by any means hurt you. Notwithstanding in this rejoice not, that

the spirits are subject unto you; but rather rejoice, because your names are written in heaven.

—LUKE 10:19–20

But ye shall receive power, after that the Holy Ghost is come upon you: and ye shall be witnesses unto me both in Jerusalem, and in all Judaea, and in Samaria, and unto the uttermost part of the earth.

—ACTS 1:8

For I am not ashamed of the gospel of Christ: for it is the power of God unto salvation to every one that believeth; to the Jew first, and also to the Greek.

—ROMANS 1:16

Now to him that is of power to establish you according to my gospel, and the preaching of Jesus Christ, according to the revelation of the mystery, which was kept secret since the world began.

—ROMANS 16:25

That your faith should not stand in the wisdom of men, but in the power of God.

—1 CORINTHIANS 2:5

For the kingdom of God is not in word, but in power.

—1 CORINTHIANS 4:20

And what is the exceeding greatness of his power to us-ward who believe, according to the working of his mighty power, Which he wrought in Christ, when he raised him from the dead, and set him at his own right hand in the heavenly places, Far above all principality, and power, and might, and dominion, and every name that is named, not only in this world, but also in that which is to come: And hath put all things under his feet, and gave him to be the head over all things to the church, Which is his body, the fulness of him that filleth all in all.

—EPHESIANS 1:19–23

These are but a few of the scriptures God gave us to know that we can always succeed. If we were to put this in the natural realm, what investor would not like to start a business with every guarantee that they would be able to always win, always beat their competition? We must understand this: we can't lose. We have the power to win every time! This is not because of anything we have done, but because of what Jesus has done. It's Jesus! How unfortunate it is that we most often have chosen to do nothing and not compete at all or simply succumb at the first little test. It is bad enough that we fail a test, how much worse must it be that we didn't even know it was a test and let the devil win without even caring enough to try? We must know we are victorious in Jesus, and our pastors need to know who they are and teach us who we need to be.

> Ye are of God, little children, and have overcome them: because greater is he that is in you, than he that is in the world.
>
> —1 JOHN 4:4

Church, pastors, brothers and sisters, we cannot lose. The nation and the church is where they are because we conceded, we threw in the towel without a fight. Why? We are predestined to be successful and to always be winners. To be successful in our Father's business we must ask and find the problem and then correct our flaws, eliminate our failures, and lean on Jesus' works that have already been done for us. Why have we produced so little when we are capable of producing so much? Why are we being defeated when we are the victorious of Christ? Please understand this, how can we the church become successful without knowing why we are failing? If every time you walked out your door you ran into it and were hurt, would you just keep doing the same thing without finding out why? What has happened in the church is that we did not get the answer so we stopped going through the door. Satan now has won, we are contained and controlled. This is so important and God made it so easy for us. How can we continue being ineffective morons for Satan? Are we too stupid to know this, or just plain lazy? If we didn't know and now do, are we going to do anything? The question for the church body is this: now that we really know what being sons and daughters do in our lives, are we really going to be different and better? Simply and honestly put, are we willing to be all God wants us to be, or willing to settle for what Satan has planned for us?

We must ask ourselves and our pastors why we, the church, have continued to lose so many. We must get hold of this! Yes, we must ask our pastors why and what they are going to do. There is also the more important question: what about the we? What is our part? The first part is to get our pastors to start teaching us and directing us toward goals of souls. There is a good slogan for every church that is going to be about the Father's business, "Goals of Souls." We must be asking our pastors, "How much do you plan to produce, and how can we help?"

Pastors, what are your goals and where are your plans? God will not do what He has commanded us to do. There is a power in prayer that we have failed to even reach yet, but it is lost in our lack! We can pray for our churches to be full and sit back and wait. We can also pray for our churches to be full and go out and invite, evangelize, and be busy about God's business. Prayer plus works, as well as faith plus works, moves God. Why? God will not do until we have done our part! God is always faithful to do His part! We must have pastors in our churches that understand we are in a business, and that business is souls. Satan wants them. Jesus commanded that we go and get them! As I pointed out earlier, we must be like Jesus and do as He would do. He came to do what? We have to know this!

> He that committeth sin is of the devil; for the devil sinneth from the beginning. For this purpose the Son of God was manifested, that he might destroy the works of the devil.
>
> —1 JOHN 3:8

The purpose of our Christian life, and that of our churches and our pastors, is to destroy the works of the devil! Start by putting God in schools instead of Satan, prayers instead of alternate lifestyles! We are the head and not the tail. It is way past time we let our politicians know this: that we want to be, choose to be, and will be one nation under God! When we do anything, cast any vote to the contrary, we have joined forces with Satan. We all have failed to grasp how easy it is to go from serving God to serving Satan. God's road is straight and narrow. With one little variation in our course we are going to a different destination. Remember the verse we just read.

> The wicked shall be turned into hell, and all the nations that forget God.
>
> —PSALM 9:17

We, the church—those of us that know the truth—must be telling others in a convincing manner that this nation is headed to hell. We are leaving a nation to our children that is becoming more and more difficult to live for Jesus. We need to be more concerned with their eternal souls going to hell than taking them to the mall for their latest fad clothes. There are many times more youth dropped of at the mall on Friday and Saturday nights than taken to church. How can we have raised up such a generation of parents that the mall is more important than eternal salvation? We grade our children every step of the way in our schools without ever watching their progress in Christ. Everything else is going to burn up, everything we purchase and provide for our children will perish. Just look at our nation and our churches, they are both lost to a world of pleasure. If we just spent as much time on our youths' salvation as we do their homework, many would not spend an eternity in hell. We would need fewer jails and treatment centers and more churches. Where our treasure is, there are hearts will be. Where's our heart, church? Where's our heart, mothers and fathers? What treasures will we leave our children?

Every politician, every judge, every pastor, church, and person who has put God aside is going to hell along with the nation. Hear this and keep this as we also must understand, we are the church, we are the nation, and we must be very careful. Many of us are not on the straight road. We are to be in this world, but not of this world. Are we? Do our lives, our church, and our pastor reflect this? We must understand that all of us have fallen short. We cannot change the past, but we can, however, learn from it and change the future. We are in a business, a family business, handed down from our heavenly Father. It's the Father's business, it's His power and authority, and our business is souls.

Now I will make some others just plain mad. Everything in the church that is not about souls, or equipping saints to be about souls, is lost production, and for the most part is about entertainment. Here is the sad part: the churches have to provide an environment and service we would like. We are wrong for wanting anything except the Word of God. Some pastors are wrong for giving in to worldly programs. It has now become a standard or normal way of having church. Regardless of denomination, region, or religion, all the services are pretty much the same. That is because they have been designed to please man. If each and every one of us would really, and I mean really, be honest, we will find a hard truth. Do you leave your church service and feel better-equipped, more capable, and changed? Can I say most just leave feeling better for having been spiritually entertained?

If I am wrong, why is our country in this shape and why are more people serving Satan and going to hell than serving God and going to heaven? Stand in the checkout line at your grocery store and read the headlines on all those magazines. Turn on your radio and television and find God. Go to the public schools and find God. In fact, where do we think we can even find God anymore? Where are the pastors that should be raising up Christians that are willing and capable to make a real change and difference by taking a stand? Now, there is someone at fault here and it is you and I. There is also someone who can change this and it is also you and I. We must grow our pastors to be capable and willing to show us how to make these changes by teaching us and leading us toward God. They must be pastors that will take the body and bride of Christ on the straight road! Will the real pastors please step forward and step up to their God-given responsibilities?

Every promise in the Bible, every victory over Satan, is because of knowledge of the Word of God. "In the beginning was the Word" (John 1:1). Heavens and earth will pass away, but God's Word will remain forever. (See Matthew 24:35; Mark 13:31: and Luke 21:33.) We must demand from our pastors that we are not willing to be children of the world anymore. We must insist, even demand, from our pastors that they stop entertaining and start teaching. We must relate to them that we will be with them and we support them. Let our church services start being about equipping us for God's business, the business of souls. We can all start by going to our Bibles and just reading all of the writing in red. What were the commandments and teachings of Jesus? Read them carefully, read them as if we just might have something wrong somewhere, we might be able to improve some things, and we are going to find any problem that hinders our business. We are going to use every instruction left to us to run the business. You will literally find a different Word. It will be like a new Bible. The Word is alive because Jesus is alive, and now we are alive for Him.

Try to think differently; you are part of an inheritance, you are to run your Father's business and your Father left you a complete guide to do so. He told us exactly what He wanted done and how we were to do it. We need to understand that is what the Bible is: it is the instruction manual from our heavenly Father. The complete history and future of God's business is in the Bible. This is a real book with a difference we fail to understand: this book is actually alive. It may be made of paper and ink, purchased on sale, or found abandoned on some shelf, but it is miraculously alive. Furthermore, it will work just like our Father said it would work. We need to just simply look around us and observe everything we see. Not one thing will remain except the words in that Bible, and those words are forever. Do we comprehend that every building, road, person, every bank account and trust fund will perish and only the Word of God will remain? Nothing we have ever seen or touched will last, except the Word of God.

Jesus made it very clear that there are rewards for those who grasp and apply this. I want every reward I can get from my Father! "Well done" are the words I want to hear. If you are in agreement with me, then we as a church and nation need new priorities with goals and vision. We fail to have the vision of God for our lives. This is where we are missing these godly pastors who are so needed for these last days. Pastors please hurry, don't wait, too many are being deceived and lost. We need you now.

> For the kingdom of heaven is as a man traveling into a far country, who called his own servants, and delivered unto them his goods. And unto one he gave five talents, to another two, and to another one; to every man according to his several ability; and straightway took his journey. Then he that had received the five

talents went and traded with the same, and made them other five talents. And likewise he that had received two, he also gained other two. But he that had received one went and digged in the earth, and hid his lord's money. After a long time the lord of those servants cometh, and reckoneth with them. And so he that had received five talents came and brought other five talents, saying, Lord, thou deliveredst unto me five talents: behold, I have gained beside them five talents more. His lord said unto him, Well done, thou good and faithful servant: thou hast been faithful over a few things, I will make thee ruler over many things: enter thou into the joy of thy lord. He also that had received two talents came and said, Lord, thou deliveredst unto me two talents: behold, I have gained two other talents beside them. His lord said unto him, Well done, good and faithful servant; thou hast been faithful over a few things, I will make thee ruler over many things: enter thou into the joy of thy lord. Then he which had received the one talent came and said, Lord, I knew thee that thou art an hard man, reaping where thou hast not sown, and gathering where thou hast not strawed: And I was afraid, and went and hid thy talent in the earth: lo, there thou hast that is thine. His lord answered and said unto him, Thou wicked and slothful servant, thou knewest that I reap where I sowed not, and gather where I have not strawed: Thou oughtest therefore to have put my money to the exchangers, and then at my coming I should have received mine own with usury. Take therefore the talent from him, and give it unto him which hath ten talents. For unto every one that hath shall be given, and he shall have abundance: but from him that hath not shall be taken away even that which he hath. And cast ye the unprofitable servant into outer darkness: there shall be weeping and gnashing of teeth. When the Son of man shall come in his glory, and all the holy angels with him, then shall he sit upon the throne of his glory: And before him shall be gathered all nations: and he shall separate them one from another, as a shepherd divideth his sheep from the goats: And he shall set the sheep on his right hand, but the goats on the left.

—MATTHEW 25:14–33

Where are we and what have we done with what we have been given? Is it a natural talent, financial, or just being in a place? What has been given is not as important as what we have done or are going to do. Are we an unprofitable servant that is going to be cast into outer darkness, are we a sheep or goat? People, these are real, serious questions that we better be asking ourselves. Doing nothing when we know that we should have done something is a sin. How many of us need to be repenting on this one? I am sure most of you are not like me, as I probably miss this every week. I failed to do all I could have done, there was always more to do. It is a sin.

Let us now try to understand what, without any doubt, is the biggest problem with our pastors. Pastors will have many faults, hang-ups, and shortcomings and can be complete failures in many areas. Now I'm speaking of godly men and women called by God, real pastors. The same overwhelming problem exists in every denomination. Pastors, after all their growing and preparation to produce, hit their largest obstruction when they begin to produce: you and me!

The volunteer workforce of the body of Christ should be the greatest, hardest-working force on the planet. Getting people to help at church is as hard as getting them to tithe. The lack of tithing and workers in the body of Christ shows our very condition and standing with God. If we believe God's Word, the rewards of both are without question, and the results of not doing so are just as plain. The question previously asked must be asked again: are we just plain stupid or lazy? Pastors now need to start their messages, "Dearly stupid and lazy, as we are gathered here today." Grasp this, people, this is us—and it's as real as it gets. You say it's not true, but you know this is true! Every politician will give way to the animal rights groups, the homosexuals, and the environmentalists. These groups come in unity and in force if they do not get their way. Politicians won't give a second notice to a pastor, church, or Christian because they will not be able to raise enough support for their cause to make a ripple. We all know this is true! Our country is headed to hell and it's because every unmoral vote cast was a part of Satan's agenda and we the church did little or nothing. We didn't even try to support the few who were trying. We better be praying that God's mercy doesn't run short, or every one of us lazy, do-nothing children of the world will surely burn in hell. It is what we deserve!

If we really understood this, if it was about what we deserved instead of God's mercy and grace, we would understand the gift Jesus gave us. If we were to grasp the reality of this, we would be flooding our pastors' offices and asking, "What are we going to do? What can I do?"

These are the conversations that are missing in all of our churches! When have we heard, "Come on pastor, we are not only behind you but some of us are up here in front, and we are helping make a way for our servant of God." When have we heard, "Don't be concerned, pastor, those that are not here are back at the church in prayer and fasting. And guess what pastor, God showed up just as we got here." When we start giving pastors that kind of congregation, we will start taking back what God has for us and what Satan has stolen.

Instead of being a generation that expanded the kingdom of God, we have more than failed. The worst decline in morality and righteousness has occurred on our watch. We are the generation that lost the most and did it in the shortest amount of time. That's us, folks. We have become "we the people of the world," instead of standing as sons and daughters of the most high God. Our generation lost more to Satan than every generation since Adam. This did not happen because we didn't really understand. It happened because we no longer care enough to do anything about it. Besides our personal shortcomings, which are usually wrapped up in "What about me?," we were not taught the real Word of God. Let us grow church bodies where the pastor can give us the real Word of God. We must have grown pastors capable and secure in their relationship with God and not some body of a church. These pastors that we need in this time will know who they really work for. These pastors will fear their Boss.

> The fear of the LORD is the beginning of knowledge: but fools despise wisdom and instruction.
>
> —PROVERBS 1:7

God is beginning to raise up some of His pastors, as well as change those knowing and willing pastors that are already in place. We the body of Christ must embrace these changes, welcome them, and encourage our pastors to step out and step in to the will of God for their lives and those of their flocks. We must get on God's side and stand against these worldly influences as well as our own desires. People, we all know change is hard. We are creatures of habit, but we can't miss this one. I believe we are about to usher in the last revival, a great revival, before the return of our Lord. We must be a help and not a hindrance. We must be for and not against. We must know and understand this great verse in God's Word. There is no middle ground, we are either on Jesus' side or Satan's side.

> He that is not with me is against me; and he that gathereth not with me scattereth abroad.
> —MATTHEW 12:30

To be a gatherer for our Lord we must get the Word of God in us and apply it. To become gatherers successful in using what has been given to us to do, we must uncover and reveal all hindrances so every problem can be fixed. There is so much missing in the body of Christ, and problems abound. We need unity as a body and a relationship with Jesus, so much so that we are like Him. We do not have an easy task. It will not be a short work, and we will have to fight Satan along the way. As much as we have to do with as many problems as we already have, it seems overwhelming, and it is, in the natural. It is now time for the supernatural workforce of God to go to work.

> Let your light so shine before men, that they may see your good works, and glorify your Father which is in heaven.
> —MATTHEW 5:16

> If thy whole body therefore be full of light, having no part dark, the whole shall be full of light, as when the bright shining of a candle doth give thee light.
> —LUKE 11:36

> For ye were sometimes darkness, but now are ye light in the Lord: walk as children of light: (For the fruit of the Spirit is in all goodness and righteousness and truth;) Proving what is acceptable unto the Lord. And have no fellowship with the unfruitful works of darkness, but rather reprove them.
> —EPHESIANS 5:8–11

The world should be seeing the manifested presence of Jesus in the body of Christ. The churches should be setting an example that the people would want to be a part of. There should be a difference in the Christians that the world can clearly see. We should be standing out as an example of what Jesus does in us. We, however, just blend in and become a part of the world. We expect our pastors to win the world without our help. In fact, it's almost in spite of us. There are a lot of people who will die and go to hell by using the excuse of how the church did this and that. Many times if it was not for this excuse, it would have been for another. We must, however, understand that the Christians that attend church have driven away well-meaning people as well, who just did not see any good in them. How can we expect our pastors and churches to win souls when the people see no benefit in Christianity? Each and every one of us needs to ask ourselves how good have I personally advertised and marketed being a Christian? How many people have decided they needed what we have?

The Christian life should be a life that the whole world envies. What the world has seen the most of is a useless religion with lost heathens that profess to be Christians. How could they not, as they are not seeing those of us that should be seen doing something that imitates Jesus.

Would it not be wonderful to have some great men of God that would say: "No! I am not Jesus, but I do act like Him." "Yes, I am doing His works, but I am not the Christ. However, please do understand He is in Me." Or, "Yes, you can see the Father and Son in me, but I am just a man like you."

Again, we are a business that must promote a product to get the desired results and meet our objectives. How do we each personally display Jesus in us? A lot of businesses have conventions to display their products, putting them under lights and demonstrating their benefits to the world. What is the product we have displayed? How has Christianity been displayed?

In the previous paragraphs, I spoke of getting businesses to help the church with the importance from their prospective. Let's look at the church in a different light, as if it were a business or organization that wants to succeed. What do we have to show people that would encourage them to invest in the purchase of the Christian life? What do we have that is worth the cost? Where is the value, the stimulation that would provoke one to purchase our product? Where are we compared to our competition? Just what is the perceived benefit of the result of using our product? Is the product desirable and wanted? The bottom line is simply this: what is the value of our product in real terms? When the perceived cost is not worth the perceived value, it is simply not marketable. Is your Christianity marketable, as seen in the eyes of others?

It should be so desirable that people are waiting in line for us to get to them. Here is the sad fact, we see people standing in lines for hours, sometimes days for some of Satan's events, for a few quick moments of excitement. If we were truly showing what God can do in us, we would have lines at our churches.

Some churches think they have arrived at some successful plateau because they have two or maybe even three services on Sunday. We need to get real; we need twenty-four hour churches, with shifts working around the clock to be able to serve the people. We can buy sex, drugs, alcohol, and most all of Satan's products twenty-four-hours a day, seven days a week. Satan has a huge market running wide open; why not Christ? The answer is because we have not given the world a product worth the cost. The fact is Satan now has achieved a greater market share by appearing more appealing. He is simply a better bargain.

If we were just walking in the gifts of God, we would have developed a huge market share. There is no other product that offers eternal life. There is also the fact that it is a gift, freely given. If we would only represent to the world the magnificent life we can have, people would be craving it and not drugs. We have been given the example of Christ's life and imparted with the knowledge and power to be like Jesus. What happened? Where are the pastors with the answers?

> The thief cometh not, but for to steal, and to kill, and to destroy: I am come that they might have life, and that they might have it more abundantly. I am the good shepherd: the good shepherd giveth his life for the sheep.
>
> —JOHN 10:10–11

Now unto him that is able to do exceeding abundantly above all that we ask or think, according to the power that worketh in us.
—EPHESIANS 3:20

But the fruit of the Spirit is love, joy, peace, longsuffering, gentleness, goodness, faith.
—GALATIANS 5:22

And the LORD shall make thee the head, and not the tail; and thou shalt be above only, and thou shalt not be beneath; if that thou hearken unto the commandments of the LORD thy God, which I command thee this day, to observe and to do them.
—DEUTERONOMY 28:13

We can and must change this. There is going to be a revival and it needs to start with each one of us individually. Can I tell you that if you would act more like Jesus, it would help me act more like Jesus? If you helped me and I helped you and then someone else saw us and joined, how long would it take to make a difference? That difference would be so dramatic that it would change the world and save untold thousands of souls. We would have envious lives, a desirable and marketable product allowing us to succeed in our Father's business.

And the Lord said, Who then is that faithful and wise steward, whom his lord shall make ruler over his household, to give them their portion of meat in due season? Blessed is that servant, whom his lord when he cometh shall find so doing. Of a truth I say unto you, that he will make him ruler over all that he hath. But and if that servant say in his heart, My lord delayeth his coming; and shall begin to beat the menservants and maidens, and to eat and drink, and to be drunken; The lord of that servant will come in a day when he looketh not for him, and at an hour when he is not aware, and will cut him in sunder, and will appoint him his portion with the unbelievers. And that servant, which knew his lord's will, and prepared not himself, neither did according to his will, shall be beaten with many stripes. But he that knew not, and did commit things worthy of stripes, shall be beaten with few stripes. For unto whomsoever much is given, of him shall be much required: and to whom men have committed much, of him they will ask the more. I am come to send fire on the earth; and what will I, if it be already kindled? But I have a baptism to be baptized with; and how am I straitened till it be accomplished!

—LUKE 12:42–50

Reread verse 49: "*I am come to send fire.*" We must understand and have this fire, as we are to be the spreader of the flame. John the Baptist told us about the fire, as well as Jesus. Let us judge ourselves. Where is our fire? Where are the "on-fire" pastors and the "on-fire" congregations? How can we set a world on fire, spreading flames, if we do not have it ourselves? In fact, for the most part we are not even warm.

First and foremost, we must grow pastors that are on fire for God. It does not make a difference of what, pastors cannot give that which they do not have. Grow pastors that are on fire! If your pastor is not on fire, send him to where he will catch the fire. Just as you cannot get from your pastor that which he does not have, he also must get it somewhere. This is not always the case, however, most of the time pastors receive from others; they seldom get it on their own. They need to be fed and imparted into, just as we do.

I indeed baptize you with water unto repentance: but he that cometh after me is mightier than I, whose shoes I am not worthy to bear: he shall baptize you with the Holy Ghost, and with fire.

—MATTHEW 3:11

Jesus told us what He was going to do when He left. Every word Jesus spoke is true. So we know this is true also, it is ours to have and use for His glory.

And I will pray the Father, and he shall give you another Comforter, that he may abide with you for ever; Even the Spirit of truth; whom the world cannot receive, because it seeth him not, neither knoweth him: but ye know him; for he dwelleth with you, and shall be in you. I will not leave you comfortless: I will come to you. Yet a little while, and the world seeth me no more; but ye see me: because I live, ye shall live also. At that day ye shall know that I am in my Father, and ye in me, and I in you. He that hath my commandments, and keepeth them, he it is that loveth me: and he that loveth me shall be loved of my Father, and I will love him, and will manifest myself to him. Judas saith unto him, not Iscariot, Lord, how is it that thou wilt manifest thyself unto us, and not unto the world? Jesus answered and said unto him, If a man love me, he will keep my words: and my Father will love him, and we will come unto him, and make our abode with him. He that loveth me not keepeth not my sayings: and the word which ye hear is not mine, but the Father's which sent me. These things have I spoken unto you, being yet present with you. But the Comforter, which is the Holy Ghost, whom the Father will send in my name, he shall teach you all things, and bring all things to your remembrance, whatsoever I have said unto you.

—JOHN 14:16–26

Jesus said in His own words that He would send another comforter. Make sure we read this well. Another comforter means He would not leave us alone. We should all know the time and event when this comforter came, as so wonderfully expressed in the Book of Acts. It is important to realize we are not alone. Today, in this very minute that you are reading this book, you are not alone; there is a presence and power with you. Like all of Jesus' words this is true also.

And when the day of Pentecost was fully come, they were all with one accord in one place. And suddenly there came a sound from heaven as of a rushing mighty wind, and it filled all the house where they were sitting. And there appeared unto them cloven tongues like as of fire, and it sat upon each of them. And they were all filled with the Holy Ghost, and began to speak with other tongues, as the Spirit gave them utterance.

—ACTS 2:1–4

This fire or the Holy Ghost is what is needed in the body of Christ. One of the worst things that has ever happened in the churches was when we allowed Satan to divide us because of the Holy Ghost. There is a great division among the churches about the Holy Ghost. We should all be able to agree that there is not to be a division in the body of

Christ. We all should be able to agree that the Holy Ghost is the Spirit of God and would not cause any divisions in the body of His Christ. If you can't agree with this you must get into the Word of God. One church, one body, one God, and when they are in unity and agreement there is power from God!

> Behold, how good and how pleasant it is for brethren to dwell together in unity! It is like the precious ointment upon the head, that ran down upon the beard, even Aaron's beard: that went down to the skirts of his garments; As the dew of Hermon, and as the dew that descended upon the mountains of Zion: for there the LORD commanded the blessing, even life for evermore.
>
> —PSALM 133

We all should be able to agree that the Holy Ghost is the worker, or the performer, of God's Word. The works of the Holy Ghost are evident in Genesis. Mary's pregnancy was by the Holy Ghost, and it was seen throughout the ministries of the apostles. He is the part of the Trinity that actually dwells in us, and we are to become the temple of His residency. Every church who is purchased by the blood of Christ baptizes in the name of the Father, Son, and Holy Ghost. We all believe that the indwelling of the Holy Ghost will change our hearts and lives and help us and strengthen us. Thank God that He does, or none would be saved. We would all lose our way. We should all be able to agree that the Holy Ghost will dwell in us and will change us. Many may think of this as a really active conscience, but we must know it is God speaking to us and be obedient to that voice.

> And after the earthquake a fire; but the LORD was not in the fire: and after the fire a still small voice.
>
> —1 KINGS 19:12

> My sheep hear my voice, and I know them, and they follow me.
>
> —JOHN 10:27

> Behold, I stand at the door, and knock: if any man hear my voice, and open the door, I will come in to him, and will sup with him, and he with me. To him that overcometh will I grant to sit with

me in my throne, even as I also overcame, and am set down with my Father in his throne. He that hath an ear, let him hear what the Spirit saith unto the churches.

—REVELATION 3:20–22

These are a few of the scriptures that are relatively clear, so what is the problem? The problem is in the same place that the answer is. I previously stated how businesses find problems to get answers, to become better. Let's start with the problem— and I am going to try to be extremely direct, if this book does anything, my prayer is that we as the body of Christ get this part—the divisional problem is the gifts of the Holy Ghost. Are they for today or have they died out? Is the use of any of these gifts today from God or Satan? We walk around these issues, not working together, with both sides being dogmatic that they have the truth. The hijackers who flew the planes into the Twin Towers did so believing they had the truth. We all, I'm sure, agree their truth was a lie. They and many others had been deceived by Satan. Here is the real truth, it's true because God said it, and the Holy Ghost is the Spirit of truth.

Even the Spirit of truth; whom the world cannot receive, because it seeth him not, neither knoweth him: but ye know him; for he dwelleth with you, and shall be in you.

—JOHN 14:17

These are Jesus' words and we must be very careful and understand what He is telling us. The Holy Ghost is the Spirit of truth and the world cannot receive Him or even know Him. It is the heathens, the lost, that we are to be saving that do not know, nor can they know, this Spirit. However, we the Christians are to know Him, for He dwelleth in us. I ask you to try to forget what you think you know. Forget your preconceived ideas of who is wrong and who is right. Let me help you here, because you have already decided that you already know the truth, right? For one, I doubt it, but I hope you do. Secondly, no matter which denomination or stance you take, you are right. How can that be? God did it His way, not man's way. So again, please forget what you think you know and just let God's Word and God's plan come alive in you.

Pray now that the Spirit of the living God, the Holy Ghost, will bring to you the truth for your life. Pray that you are in His will for your life, that understanding and knowledge will be imparted to you according to God's plan and that your mind will be receptive and your life reflective of His will. In Jesus' name, amen.

Let us start with what Jesus said about the Holy Ghost:

> Wherefore I say unto you, All manner of sin and blasphemy shall be forgiven unto men: but the blasphemy against the Holy Ghost shall not be forgiven unto men. And whosoever speaketh a word against the Son of man, it shall be forgiven him: but whosoever speaketh against the Holy Ghost, it shall not be forgiven him, neither in this world, neither in the world to come. Either make the tree good, and his fruit good; or else make the tree corrupt, and his fruit corrupt: for the tree is known by his fruit. O generation of vipers, how can ye, being evil, speak good things? for out of the abundance of the heart the mouth speaketh. A good man out of the good treasure of the heart bringeth forth good things: and an evil man out of the evil treasure bringeth forth evil things. But I say unto you, That every idle word that men shall speak, they shall give account thereof in the day of judgment. For by thy words thou shalt be justified, and by thy words thou shalt be condemned.
>
> —MATTHEW 12:31–37

We are told as directly as possible that blasphemy against the Holy Ghost shall not be forgiven. So we must always take this very seriously. Also, we should be aware of what blasphemy is. The Random House Webster's Second Edition Dictionary says of it: "To speak irreverently about God or sacred things." We all should take care of what we say about the Holy Ghost, as well as any other thing of God, for that matter. "For by thy words thou shalt be justified" (v. 37). The other important part of these verses is very simple: we are either good or corrupt. The line between good and corrupt is so thin that we can cross and not know it. We must always beware that we are walking the narrow road.

To make sure we stay in God's will, we will stay in God's Word. Let's look at these so divisive verses, the chapter and verses that have caused so many problems.

The different positions or interpretations have gone to the extreme, with one side saying it is of Satan and the other side stating that if it's not their way, we aren't saved. To those extremists, I will simply ask—revisit your position, and do so in love of our fellow man. Know that division is and never will be of God.

Read these scriptures carefully, as if for the first time:

> Now concerning spiritual gifts, brethren, I would not have you ignorant. Ye know that ye were Gentiles, carried away unto these dumb idols, even as ye were led. Wherefore I give you to understand, that no man speaking by the Spirit of God calleth Jesus accursed: and that no man can say that Jesus is the Lord, but by the Holy Ghost. Now there are diversities of gifts, but the same Spirit. And there are differences of administrations, but the same Lord. And there are diversities of operations, but it is the same God which worketh all in all. But the manifestation of the Spirit is given to every man to profit withal. For to one is given by the Spirit the word of wisdom; to another the word of knowledge by the same Spirit; To another faith by the same Spirit; to another the gifts of healing by the same Spirit; To another the working of miracles; to another prophecy; to another discerning of spirits; to another divers kinds of tongues; to another the interpretation of tongues: But all these worketh that one and the selfsame Spirit, dividing to every man severally as he will. For as the body is one, and hath many members, and all the members of that one body, being many, are one body: so also is Christ. For by one Spirit are we all baptized into one body, whether we be Jews or Gentiles, whether we be bond or free; and have been all made to drink into one Spirit. For the body is not one member, but many. If the foot shall say, Because I am not the hand, I am not of the body; is it therefore not of the body? And if the ear shall say, Because I am not the eye, I am not of the body; is it therefore not of the body? If the whole body were an eye, where were the hearing? If the whole were hearing, where the smelling? But now hath God set the members every one of them in the body, as it hath pleased him. And if they were all one member, where were the body? But now are they many members, yet but one body. And the eye cannot say unto the hand, I have no need of thee: nor again the head

to the feet, I have no need of you. Nay, much more those members of the body, which seem to be more feeble, are necessary: And those members of the body, which we think to be less honourable, upon these we bestow more abundant honour; and our uncomely parts have more abundant comeliness. For our comely parts have no need: but God hath tempered the body together, having given more abundant honour to that part which lacked. That there should be no schism in the body; but that the members should have the same care one for another. And whether one member suffer, all the members suffer with it; or one member be honoured, all the members rejoice with it. Now ye are the body of Christ, and members in particular. And God hath set some in the church, first apostles, secondarily prophets, thirdly teachers, after that miracles, then gifts of healings, helps, governments, diversities of tongues. Are all apostles? are all prophets? are all teachers? are all workers of miracles? Have all the gifts of healing? do all speak with tongues? do all interpret? But covet earnestly the best gifts: and yet shew I unto you a more excellent way.

—1 CORINTHIANS 12

Let us review these with the love of Christ and the mind of Christ, in unity of one bride-to-be. I pray we all gain clarity as we spend some time reviewing these scriptures. One of the key points I would like to bring to light is my belief that none of us need to change what God has called us to be. I also believe that neither do the positions of our church doctrine need to be changed. We just need to accept God's Word, God's works, and each other as brothers and sisters. Please, in the name of Jesus, if not for our lives, than for the lives being lost because of the division in the churches, rethink these issues. I am going to spend some time on breaking this down in hopes it may bring some clarity. The key point will be that none of us has to change what God has called us to be; neither do we need to change the spiritual or religious positions of our churches. What we need to do, every last one of us, is accept God and God's works in the body of Christ.

Verses 1–3 give us some great insight. First of all, Paul did not want us to be ignorant. The sound advice he gave is still for us today. He tells the early church what they were and how they were led. It is not much different than today. We have so many things leading us in the wrong direction these days. For instances, there are idols of financial power, objects, alcohol, drugs, sex, and pornography, to name but a few influences.

We are given by Paul understanding that no man can say Jesus is Lord, but by the Holy Ghost. Some have said this means if you're not speaking in tongues, you're not saved. They are the unlearned—of whom we need to be aware; for they serve Satan and not God.

Verse 30 clearly shows us we are not all to speak in tongues. Neither are we to have all of the gifts. Even with the best of intentions, if we misinterpret God's Word, we miss God and find Satan. Please understand that this seemingly minor misinterpretation always heads us straight toward Satan, always!

Verses 4–7 are very important. Now, church, here is the problem and the answer to the problem. Let's get this one right. "There are diversities of gifts...differences of administrations...[and] diversities of operations." God's Word says there are to be differences and diversities. What is our problem?

The problem is we can't accept someone who is different. We can't accept that another church does it differently than our church. We are right, and they have to be wrong. These positions are of the immature Christian who does not understand the power of God.

We then come to verses 8–11, which tell us of the gifts of the Holy Ghost. The big question dividing us is: were these gifts only for a time and not active today? The answer is *yes!* Are we to have and use these gifts of the Holy Ghost today? The answer is *yes!*

How can both be right? We think this can't be, but I believe it is because it is of God! We must, every one of us, get away from the natural and get into the supernatural by walking with God. We need to be doing what God needs us to do with what God set in place for us to do it. Now please understand, that does not mean every church has to be charismatic! God has set in place all of us with our differences and diversities. He has given each church the gifts He wants them to have.

We all must understand that to work with God we must join Him in another place. Never can we work with God in the natural; God never has neither will He ever operate in the natural. We must understand this principle. I have no idea how many ways there are to build a universe, but my God did it supernaturally. Man was created supernaturally as well as woman. I can think of many ways God could have come to earth from heaven, but my Savior chose an impossible virgin birth. It was not natural; it was supernatural. He returned to the right hand of the Father exactly the same way, supernaturally. I do not understand all of it, but this much I am sure of, when we want to work with God, we must get out of the natural and start working in the supernatural.

We are a very well-educated society with highly advanced medical knowledge, so much so that the world comes to America for treatment. We all now know about germs and diseases and have been educated as to how doctors heal. The people laid on the streets waiting for the shadow of Peter to fall on them and they we healed. Dr. Luke was around, and I am so glad he did not tell everyone that shadows cannot heal, or that it can't be done that way. Working with God is always a supernatural experience. God himself said, "I change not" (Mal. 3:6). Is that true?

Verses 8–18 show us God's idea and plan for a body. This is the body of Christ. We are one body, but with different members. The important thing is verse 18. Read this again with a better understanding of God!

> But now hath God set the members every one of them in the body, as it hath pleased him.
> —1 CORINTHIANS 12:18

We must understand that God has made and set into place the body of His Son, the body that is to be the bride of Christ. God did it and it pleased Him.

Verses 18–26 will clearly tell any of us that if we keep an open mind, there are many different and diverse members that God has tempered into one body—a body that is not to have any schism or differences. Is it right to speak in tongues? Yes, if you were called by God to do so. Is it right to be in a church that does not speak in tongues? Yes, if you were called by God to be in that church. We must follow the leading of the Holy Ghost as to where we are to be and what gifts we are to have. They are gifts, and not all gifts are given to all. The most important thing that I believe we need to know about is to accept what God gives us and to accept, as well, those who have gifts other than ours. The mentality of "I don't have it and it's not taught or practiced in my church, so it's wrong" is not the mind of Christ. It is important that we each ask ourselves serious questions if we are serious about our stand with God. If we do not have the mind of Christ, why? And whose mind do we have? Each of us as individuals must answer this, it is an eternal question of great importance.

> That there should be no schism in the body; but that the members should have the same care one for another.
>
> —1 CORINTHIANS 12:25

Here is the answer, we are all different but there is to be no difference in the body of Christ, we should care one for another.

This chapter ends with some great advice:

> But covet earnestly the best gifts: and yet shew I unto you a more excellent way.
>
> —1 CORINTHIANS 12:31

Let each of us have the freedom to covet what is best for us as individuals and as denominations or parts of the body of Christ. You must trust in God's Word for Him to show "unto you a more excellent way." I believe this has started, and we are ready to begin the process of becoming one body. The church must look at its accomplishments in the last fifty years by acknowledging that, in many areas, we have fallen way short of our mark. We must be wise enough to see that Jesus gave us some great words and we must see the truth in them.

> And Jesus knew their thoughts, and said unto them, Every kingdom divided against itself is brought to desolation; and every city or house divided against itself shall not stand.
>
> —MATTHEW 12:25

We cannot stand if we are divided. We are a family of God that needs to come together in love and oneness. Sometimes we simply must understand that our part is to heal and come together in unity. We all have played a part in separating ourselves. We can take any denomination for an example. I'm going to use the Baptists because I have so many wonderful Baptist friends and I can trust I'll be forgiven. In the divisive manner we have experienced in the past, the Baptists have not been willing to work with or even consider the ministry of someone who is Pentecostal. Baptist and all others, you're wrong for being that way. Being baptized in the Holy Ghost and speaking in tongues, as well as walking in other gifts, is real to that part of the body of Christ and is of God. Many of us find this hard to accept. Believe me, there is nothing in God's Word that says any of the gifts will diminish! Nor is there anything that says not having them changes one's salvation position. I know there is nothing in the Word of God that says it will end. In fact, it says that in the last days God is going to pour out His spirit. Let's just believe God and accept our brothers and sisters in Christ. Sight is real to the eye, but the ear only hears. We are the same body, and both are important. In defense of the Baptist, the Pentecostals have been demonstrating the power of the Holy Ghost, speaking in tongues, and falling when slain in the Spirit. Pentecostals, what have you accomplished?

> If any man among you seem to be religious, and bridleth not his tongue, but deceiveth his own heart, this man's religion is vain.
> —JAMES 1:26

> Even so the tongue is a little member, and boasteth great things. Behold, how great a matter a little fire kindleth! And the tongue is a fire, a world of iniquity: so is the tongue among our members, that it defileth the whole body, and setteth on fire the course of nature; and it is set on fire of hell. For every kind of beasts, and of birds, and of serpents, and of things in the sea, is tamed, and hath been tamed of mankind: But the tongue can no man tame; it is an unruly evil, full of deadly poison.
> —JAMES 3:5–8

Is speaking in tongues real? Yes, to the part of the body God has set in place to do so. It has a place of importance, and that place should never be to divide the body of Christ. Paul who tells us not to be ignorant also says:

> Yet in the church I had rather speak five words with my understanding, that by my voice I might teach others also, than ten thousand words in an unknown tongue.
>
> —1 CORINTHIANS 14:19

Which side is wrong? Both! Which side is right? Both! Which side are we to be on? God's side! There is only one side and we need to be sure we are on it. We need to understand: God does not have sides, He just has family, sons, and daughters! Come on church let's get out of the box, let's step up to God, and let's work supernaturally. I need for everyone to understand something about stepping up to God: no matter how you go to Jerusalem you always have to go up. We need to understand this is a place God always is—up.

Here is what I think, please understand I am now away from God's words, which are always true, and writing Ron's thoughts. This is just plain food for thought. What I believe should have been the Pentecostal part is the ears of the church body since they are able to hear the small, still voice so very clearly. Instead, the ear tried to be the mouth by proclaiming worldly values instead of God's values. Instead of being able to tell the body of Christ what God is speaking today, the church tuned out the message because of the messenger. The Baptists, as an example of all other denominations, were to be the arm of God. Reaching out to the world with the good news. The fact is that the Baptists have done and continue to do an admirable job in the mission field. They are performing today as the Catholics did in the early church. Just think what we would be able to do together as one hearing, reaching, healing, and restoring church! We would be saving souls in greater numbers than we can even imagine. We would have twenty-four-hour church.

I pray that we can learn to hear the voice of God and receive it in oneness, undefiled from whomever God is using at the time. I pray we can accept that those who are Pentecostal are a part, just as every denomination is a part. Each part is set in place by God and it pleases God.

I end with these thoughts. You need to be where God has placed you! It is not important which denomination, and it's not important whether you are charismatic or not. What is important is that you are the best at what God has called for you to be—family!

> Now I say, That the heir, as long as he is a child, differeth nothing from a servant, though he be lord of all; But is under tutors and governors until the time appointed of the father. Even so we, when we were children, were in bondage under the elements of the world: But when the fulness of the time was come, God sent forth his Son, made of a woman, made under the law, To redeem them that were under the law, that we might receive the adoption of sons. And because ye are sons, God hath sent forth the Spirit of his Son into your hearts, crying, Abba, Father. Wherefore thou art no more a servant, but a son; and if a son, then an heir of God through Christ.
>
> —GALATIANS 4:1–7

Amen.

Chapter Eight

GLORY OF GOD'S CREATION

We all are privileged to see the glory of God's creation almost every day. Most never stop to appreciate it or even notice. When we simply look at the sky at night with all the stars and wake up the next day to look at our sun, we hardly ever take the time to recognize just how amazing it really is. We must understand the authority and power of His spoken Word. God set the name of Jesus above every name, and we need to come into the place of kinship and power that God has provided for us if we are to serve in and work in His supernatural power!

> And God said, Let there be light: and there was light. And God saw the light, that it was good: and God divided the light from the darkness.
>
> —GENESIS 1:3–4

There were trillions upon countless trillions of cubic miles of materials, specifically mostly hydrogen and helium that were put together at a density of 150 times that of water. The enormous size alone is enough to suggest Creation and a Creator. Now add the fact that the power is the equivalent of the explosions of 100 billion 1-megaton hydrogen bombs. Yes—billions! This enormous amount of power, if it was the total expended since day one, or even yearly, would be immense. It is, however, the power expended every second of every day. We call it the sun; science calls it a star—one of thousands. The temperature alone is 29 million degrees Fahrenheit. Yes, that is millions. What is the power of our God if He can simply speak something like this into existence? We are not even capable of understanding His real power, let alone the very nature of our God. Can we ever imagine how it will be when there is no sun and only the glory of God lights our world? Glory of Himself, that which is literally God will light the heavens!

> And the city had no need of the sun, neither of the moon, to shine in it: for the glory of God did lighten it, and the Lamb is the light thereof.
>
> —REVELATION 21:23

"The Lamb is the light thereof," what a wonderful thing it will be to see this. No shadows, no darkness, and no Satan, only the light of our Savior, Lord, and King.

The sun created by God is the light of this world now. We should be able to see the correlation—that every living thing on this earth is dependent on the sun for its life. Every soul on this earth is dependent upon the Son for their lives. The plant that is able to get more of the sun is the plant that grows the biggest, is the healthiest, and produces the most fruit. Many plants move as the sun revolves over the earth, following the sun. Wouldn't it be wonderful if we humans would simply follow the Son, as the plants and leaves follow the sun? The leaf on that weed in the yard, following the natural instinct placed in it, does better than we humans with all the prophets and the Bible to guide and direct us! Think about it!

Our pastoral trees must be following the Son. Their lives must reflect the life-giving rays of the Son. They must be like leaves turning as needed to get as much as possible of the sun everyday. Every living being is dependent on the sun and the fact that it will shine on a regular basis.

The amount of regularity is also important. We would not have a very productive growing season if the sun were to shine just once in a while. If the sun were to shine for a solid week, day and night, and then not for three weeks, most things would become sickly and die. Likewise, pastors without a regular and substantial dwelling with God also will become sickly and die. There are no substitutes that can provide this needed nourishment. They simply do not get enough Son, especially not on a regular basis! Pastors must set some limits. They must manage their time, so that they can bask in the Son. We all want to be ministered to by a pastor who is a regular Son-bather—well-tanned, and having been warmed to the core by the Son's wonderful rays of warmth. Churches must get this, we as individuals must get this, and pastors themselves must get this! Pastors cannot have stored up enough "Son" that they can enter into the ministry and keep giving without receiving! It is always imperative that pastors still spend time, not only *in* the Son, but more so, time *with* the Son.

We have many sick, dying, unproductive churches simply for this reason: their pastors ran out of Son. Church, when a pastor, and that includes every one of our pastors, run out of Son they begin to run on the natural, which is the worldly. Many churches and pastors just slipped from spiritual to worldly, and did so without even noticing the change or understanding the reason. Many of us have experienced this, and almost every time missed the signs until it was too late. Out of respect and love for our pastor, we just accepted the missed areas of neglect as being busy, having other priorities, and an assortment of other excuses. When we look back we see what happened, we are all at fault when this happens. We must be watching out as well as over all of our pastoral staff and not just the senior pastor.

If your pastor has no regular time specifically set aside to study and to be in prayer, and also to hear from God for his life and the church's direction, insist that they do. Every church also needs to be sending their pastor and his/her spouse to several events to be uplifted and encouraged and to further educate themselves. I have used the analogy of a tree for pastors and it is a great comparison. Here is another point that makes this analogy so real to our pastors. In great storms, and even hurricanes, the forests receive little or no damage. When the winds of Satan blow so hard the trees start to lean. They just lean on the one that is next to them and that tree leans on the one next to it. As a forest, as a whole and in unity, they all withstand the storms. The same trees, standing by themselves or in small groups, fall. We must provide for our pastors something on which to lean! We also must learn that as a church, we need to be one forest learning to lean on one another!

Does your pastor have younger children at home? If so, when was the last time your congregation got together and sent your pastor and spouse out to dinner and a movie, complete with a babysitter provided? Many times there are offers to take the pastors to dinner and that's great, however, let us also send them by themselves! How about sending them off on a three-day weekend, complete with babysitter and guest speaker to minister in their absence? We all need to be aware of the needs of the pastor's spouse also. Many times they are forgotten. However, they play a significant role not only in the pastor's life, but in the success of the church. There must be times that these couples are sent to a quiet place alone, simply to rest and restore themselves. They have a marriage, a relationship that must have time and attention also! Let us honor the spouses as well as we do the pastors.

> And on the seventh day God ended his work which he had made; and he rested on the seventh day from all his work which he had made.
>
> —GENESIS 2:2

> And there appeared an angel unto him from heaven, strengthening him.
>
> —LUKE 22:43

God may not sleep, according to Scripture, however it's evident that He rests. Jesus, before going to the cross, was strengthened by angels. How can we expect more from our pastors? Every pastor needs to be working and busy about the Father's business, and we should expect hardworking pastors with good work ethics and practices. We need to be removing lazy pastors from every church. If they are not producing, dig and dung first! If they still do not produce, follow Jesus' words and get rid of them.

Kingdom business is too important to waste time and resources on the nonachievers. Again, this is where the business professionals in the church can help a receptive pastor. Goals, deadlines, financial planning, as well as simply managing time and people, are part of their normal routine. Most pastors and people in church management will not accept these ideas well, and it is a shame. Many in the normal church management, those helping actively in the church have a higher rate of bankruptcy and job turnover than the world. Spiritual tasks should always be left to the pastor, but many pastors should not be making financial and management decisions without a lot of help. In speaking with many great pastors, they are praying for this kind of help. Great pastors know their gifts as well as limitations. Look at how many times Jesus used fish to authenticate Himself and to feed the multitudes. Yet there is not one place in the Bible where Jesus actually caught a fish Himself. He even sent Peter to catch the fish to pay the taxes.

We expect our pastors today to build the boat, make the nets, go to the ocean, catch the fish, and upon their return clean them and cook them for dinner. We just want the fish fry! It should be a requirement that pastors be accomplishing tasks and are not just busy. Our churches are desperate for pastors that are producing fruit and not just programs. We, as the body of Christ, should no longer support program-producing pastors. We must demand production, and we know that production is souls. We also must be recognizing when good pastors are wasting their time in a bad way. Many are trying to be building planners and banquet planners, most failing at both. They are outside their calling and their area of expertise in these types of tasks.

There are those that adapt, study, and achieve a desirable outcome. However, if they spent the time it took to achieve these results on reaching the lost, restoring the hurting, and teaching their congregations that to grow in Christ is also to grow in accepting responsibilities, their church would be far ahead of where it is now. We must have pastors teaching and busy doing what needs to be done, not what we want. These are God's pastors, the others are man's.

Delegating work to a volunteer workforce is a hard thing. It becomes impossible when the pastor cannot trust his people, and when his people keep letting him down. We have discussed the many reasons this happens, earlier in this book. We have two major problems here: poor teaching from our pastors, and Christians who just will not allow themselves to be bothered too much by working for and at the church. The second problem with the people has been around forever and is not easy to solve. As I have mentioned, the doers are 8 percent of the church. We must increase this percentage. It is not acceptable and it must not be tolerated any longer. It can, however, only be solved by fixing the first problem: pastors who are not teaching us the importance of working for our Lord. These are quite simply pastors who are either poor teachers or they are satisfied with this condition, neither of which is acceptable. Not all pastors are teachers. In fact, in many instances, we need teachers gifted by God to step up and help these pastors.

Pastors set the goals, decide which battles to fight, and lead the charge. They use the troops and truly get us ready for the battles we have yet to fight. We have a war to win! The old normalcy is no longer tolerable. There is a mentality in all denominations that simply going to church on some type of a regular basis fulfills a duty to God. They are told that if they sow some money in the church fund, they will even be blessed. There is more preaching on prosperity than any other topic in our churches today, especially those on television. Good, even great preachers have had to change their priorities when they were faced with those million-dollar airtime bills. In many countries, a church could be built for the cost of a half-hour on television. I enjoy many wonderful men and women of God who are on television that I would have never been able to hear preach if not for television. I doubt, however, that for many ministries it is the best dollar value to save souls. How many thousands of churches could have been built in countries that need them for what is spent on television ministries promoting the messenger, not the message?

If businesspeople were running these ministries and counting sales of souls achieved, they would be sending in an "on foot" sales force and advertising budgets would be cut as ineffective. It cannot be working. Look at the condition of our nation, our schools, and our churches. There are more mega-churches, more money, more preachers, more airtime, and our country is still heading to hell at breakneck speed. We are failing to inspect the fruit being produced. Please understand that I am not against all television ministries. In fact, I know of several that do a tremendous amount of good. There are some who are about reaching the lost and do so not just in words, but in actions and deeds. They are producing a lot of fruit, and I commend them, and I pray God's continued blessings for them. As I mentioned, however, there are some that are all about raising up the preacher and not Jesus. It's all about the money. It should not be a surprise that they are demons from hell, imposters doing Satan's work and stealing God's money. All of this makes the teaching role of the real church harder, and makes reaching the lost even harder.

It could be stopped quickly by simply using the spirit of discernment before sending them money, and knowing the fruit being produced before allowing them to steal away from God's finances. Support the good ones after supporting your church correctly. Do so by telling ministries to show us proof of the fruit, the fruit of souls. We do not want your hype with no fruit. Become a good steward of what God has provided you to give.

It is the responsibility of everyone to see that our pastor has the time and resources to perform and accomplish everything that God would have him do. The importance of having set in place the needed time and resources to keep pastors healthy must not be overlooked, either. Many pastors are simply burned out, not even realizing when or how. They just discovered one day that they have become a remnant of what they once were. These pastors will never fulfill God's plan in their lives without a major change in the organization of their ministries.

You and I must accept responsibility and take appropriate steps to stop the terrible drain on some of our pastors. These pastors, when properly supported financially, emotionally, and spiritually by their congregations, can still turn the world upside down. The truth will be that some of these pastors are failures—plain and simple—however, for the vast majority we failed and failed them miserably. When not allowed to have proper time to study, rest, and fulfill their calling, not only do they suffer, but all of the church suffers with them. This is the condition of a great many churches today, so much so that it has become normal to us. It is not normal and we need to start seeing it for what it is; unorganized, poorly equipped, and in need of a new and revitalized workforce. We can no longer accept and neither support a nonproducing church! It is our personal responsibility to do our best for God, not a church, pastor, or denomination.

The greatest business of all humanity, as a whole, is much less organized than the hot dog sales stand on our streets. The church needs to wise up and get some great business executives involved to turn the church around like the automobile industry did a few years back. Many times the whole world of God becomes reduced to the workings inside of a four-walled church.

There is no vision, no goals, and just everyday drudgery. Reaching the lost, starting a revival, and restoring the neighborhood becomes nothing but memories of days gone by.

> Where there is no vision, the people perish: but he that keepeth the law, happy is he.
>
> —PROVERBS 29:18

Then the circle begins: the pastor's teaching, preaching, and encouragement drops off considerably. The congregation does not mature; there is almost no spiritual growth and more so, many even have regressed. This results in needful people that require lots of time and energy which now puts an even larger strain on the pastor. These needful people are a result of poor teaching and pastoring. Many times without realizing it, the church begins a spiral downward, getting progressively worse as time passes. This often starts when pastors have come to join congregations of unskilled Christians, not knowing they were not properly grown and pastored. This is also a huge problem for our new young pastors that are still growing and maturing and are not yet prepared for this. Then the truth begins to hit them, along with the workload. Their new congregation needs the pastor for everything, and there is no one else capable of helping. This condition exists all over America and in every denomination. To correct this, we must be growing some highly capable pastors that are equipped with everything God has for them. They need it all!

The fact is, many of these churches and pastors need the assistance of grown mature men and women of God to help them. We need to start looking more like a global business instead of little neighborhood mom-and-pop store. The churches that have an excess of grown disciples need to be sending and sharing them. There are many of us who sit in our churches because it is comfortable, easy, and a habit. So sadly, 92 percent of the non-doers go to church for one of two reasons: the majority go out of the habit of doing so for a long time. They go here Friday night and to church on Sundays. The others are there because they feel they are fulfilling their duty to God. They truly believe that showing up every Sunday is not only a salvation experience, but that they become part of God's family. A great many of these are not saved, and no one wants to hurt their feelings. Real pastors of God would educate this group quickly. Real pastors are pastoring sheep, not goats, and they grow wheat, not tares.

We need to be stretching ourselves and helping other struggling churches. The very large churches that have been blessed with so much talent need to send that talent to the other churches in town. They need to loan them to train and make the other local church a success also. When the body of Christ starts helping other churches across denominational lines, we are going to start gaining ground and we will start acting and looking like Jesus. I would like for every mega-church to look at this scripture as food for thought. Does it fit the profile of what they are doing?

> And he spake a parable unto them, saying, The ground of a certain rich man brought forth plentifully: and he thought within himself, saying, What shall I do, because I have no room where to bestow my fruits? And he said, This will I do: I will pull down my barns, and build greater; and there will I bestow all my fruits and my goods.
>
> —LUKE 12:16–18

Mega-churches, this is for you today! I am sure, without a doubt, that these churches understand and regularly minister on sowing and reaping, but are they? Let's say the talented, gifted, and mature Christians, who have been grown under a great and mature pastor, simply divided up their town and decided to win their market share back from Satan. What would happen if they began assisting other churches, actually doing something that would not benefit their own church? They would just simply be working for the kingdom of God with no direct return for themselves. Let's use McDonald's again. How many billions of hamburgers have they sold? What if they just kept growing their first store instead of selling franchises across the town, the country, and then the world? It would be wonderful if the church was as successful in spreading the greatest message there ever was, as the hamburger sandwich industry has been. What does that really say about the church? Jesus is the bread of life. (See John 6:35.) Is the bread of life as marketable as a hamburger? Jesus is by far the most important thing in all the world and should be the largest and fastest growing business in the world! The fast-food industry, and many others, who have learned to do the same thing, the same way, over and over again are very successful. If you're a successful church and want to act like Christ, go help the one that isn't, even if they are different. *Wow!* What a thought: churches working together as one and competing against Satan instead of just working for themselves. When will we wake up and start understanding that Christianity is God's business of souls and, when managed correctly, will outproduce every known business conceived by man.

I hope that we—you and I—have come to the realization that the church does have everything it needs to be successful and to become the great army of Christ that He would have us be! We just seldom put it all together at the same time in the same place. We are like a family that is starving to death yet has a pantry overflowing with food that just needs to be prepared and cooked. It is not hard! We have just allowed Satan to make it hard. We can and must understand this!

We must put forth our efforts where they are needed to overcome this state of spiritual starvation in our churches. Every lacking church must be because of a lack in pastoring. This must be true because there is no lack in God. If this is our church, and our pastor, we must not be blameful, we need to be thankful. How we got to this point is not the concern. The concern should now be what are we going to do together to be successful? It really makes no difference if it is because a great pastor is made ineffective by a poor congregation, or vice versa. It is ultimately the pastor's responsibility, however, they should never have to carry the load themselves without our help.

We all know that there are many in the church that will never grow. They are just trying to fulfill some sense of obligation to God, and they think that their presence in a sanctuary once a week does that. If your pastor is not teaching and raising you up to not only be on your own spiritually, but to reach others, you need to get the situation corrected immediately. You, perhaps, need a new pastor. We all need new pastors at times, and many times a new pastor is simply the result of sending your tired, stressed, overly-needed present pastor to a good retreat or conference. We need to have the foresight to send our pastors on a week-long cruise before they slide into a year-long depression. Another very effective way of getting a new pastor is by simply growing beyond the baby stage ourselves and help by giving instead of receiving. If we can grasp and implement this concept of resting and restoring our pastors, which includes the spiritual growth of ourselves, we will be having new pastors across this nation that are effective in producing an abundant crop! Then we can start being the successful businesses we should be.

Caution! We have all seen this picture: a pastor has lost something, their "zip" is missing! They are no longer enthused and they are certainly no motivator of others. We now have a new phrase for this condition. God is calling him or her elsewhere; they are being "relocated" or "replanted." Sounds good, right? This phrase makes us all feel better about ourselves, our failures, and is a much easier sell to the congregation. The next thing we know, this pastor loads up his family and moves halfway across the country, finds a new location, and goes to work. This same unproductive, worn-out pastor now has godly men and women that have been grown to help, to provide, and to do. All of the sudden, this same ineffectual pastor is doing mighty works for God. What the pastor needed was a congregation to help, a time to be refreshed, and time to be in study and prayer. This can only happen when pastors set standards, not only for themselves, but also on their availability. They must set limits, boundaries, and requirements for their congregation as well.

The pastor who is always there and always available may sound good, but will always be a nonproducing pastor. These pastors will be well-liked, great program directors, many are great cooks, and they always provide entertaining services. These pastors will not raise up missionaries or evangelists or teachers. More importantly, they will not raise up their congregation to where God is. You'll never find this pastor in a larger church, and they will never be successful fruit-producers. These are the pastors that many people want because, like all babies, they want their pacifier now and are too impatient to wait for a healthy meal. They can't feed themselves or anyone else. These pastors are simply babysitters, and become pastoral diaper changers who always have to clean up our messes. Understand, these are good men and women, wonderful neighbors, and friends that are a true joy to know and be around. The fact still remains that they are not producing the results of a kingdom business. They simply are a waste of time and finances. When will we understand the spiritual things of God and grow past the worldly things of man?

They are pastors who will spend a tremendous amount of time cooking chicken, but do not have the time to reach the lost. We all know them. In fact, how many of us are at a church with a cafeteria? Why? The truth is most of us are too fat to start with and have no need for another dinner, and if we were out knocking on doors and saving the lost, we would all be healthier and live longer. We would also expand the kingdom of heaven in the process and change our neighborhoods. Does the cafeteria receive more time, energy, and finances than evangelism? If so, close it! You'll live longer! I know this sounds completely absurd and is angering some. If this hurt your feelings, there is some good Scripture on eating at the church, however I am sure we can all agree we are doing "churchy stuff" and it is not for us.

> What? have ye not houses to eat and to drink in? or despise ye the church of God, and shame them that have not? what shall I say to you? shall I praise you in this? I praise you not.
> —1 CORINTHIANS 11:22

> And if any man hunger, let him eat at home; that ye come not together unto condemnation. And the rest will I set in order when I come.
> —1 CORINTHIANS 11:34

How many of us have a lot of meals at our workplace? The apostle Paul didn't think we needed to be eating at the Father's business office either. Am I saying it is all wrong? No, only the importance of it in almost every church has been placed far above any evangelism programs. How many churches have a well-decorated baptistry that is seldom used, behind the highly practiced and frequently rehearsed choir? Here is a shock, when did Jesus ever command us to sing? Was it right before "Go ye into all the world" or after? (See Mark 16:15.)

The really good fruit-producing pastors have the ability to see the whole picture by understanding their complete calling and putting responsibilities to God and His works above our whining, petty needs. These pastors also understand that not all pastors are teachers and were never designed by God to be. They get help where it is needed without feeling they have failed by not being all things to all people. These are the pastors that know who they are in the Lord.

Not only do they know what their calling is, but they know who called them. Mature godly pastors are not all things to all people. They understand their giftings and have true respect for the calling and giftings of others. Jealously is not a part of their ministry; they find great pleasure in the spiritual growth of others and have the common sense to use them in the fullness of God's kingdom. These are pastors who not only know how to stand, but raise up others to stand. Thank you, God, for these pastors.

> And he gave some, apostles; and some, prophets; and some, evangelists; and some, pastors and teachers.
> —Ephesians 4:11

> Are all apostles? are all prophets? are all teachers? are all workers of miracles?
> —1 Corinthians 12:29

There are some really good teaching pastors, but not all are. So, as needed, get a teacher and, praise God, let the teacher teach! In all other areas, pastors and congregations must believe God to provide good men and women to fill the other needs of God's church. God called and equipped them just as He did pastors. When we allow the other men and women to be active in our churches, the body will become complete. This must be done in unity, in order, and without jealousy. Confident pastors have allowed their churches to have great harvests because of allowing others to minister in their called areas.

We must also know we will see some really good teachers and preachers in the natural. They are highly skilled and capable of reaching many. We must recognize when these people are not spiritual. Many church bodies have been lead astray by these very good teachers and preachers. They simply do not know God's Word and are led by the world to serve men and not God. Many times they were well-meaning in trying to use their talents, but simply failed to allow God to use them. This is the pastor's responsibility, and we all should assist by making sure that anything being presented is scripturally correct.

The same goes for all of the different fivefold offices, such as the teachers. The pastor cannot and was never intended to walk in every office. In a small church just starting out, the pastor is usually the only one to lead and must be all things. Any church, however, that does not have an evangelist, a teacher, and a prophet is incomplete. These are required to grow spiritually and within the structure that God intended. I have seen churches without a good evangelist. Every one of these churches has always been about themselves and their programs.

When an evangelist speaks God's Words, God's priority, and God's timing into the body, the congregation might get upset and sometimes just plain mad. They end up rejecting God and God's plans for their church. This has been one of the most painful lessons I have ever had to learn and was, without a doubt, the hardest to learn. If your evangelist is speaking, please understand their passion and boldness. They are proclaiming what they are hearing from God. Seeing it rejected many times makes it difficult not to take it as a rejection of them. As an evangelist, I must tell you that I still cannot understand why everyone does not have my passion, and why they do not hear the same message that I do. I am lost as to how many spend so much time, energy, and money on nonessential programs. How can we do the same thing and expect a different result? Am I the only one who reads the seriousness of my Lord's position on selling in the church? Am I the only one who reads Paul's writings and sees that we should be a business and not a restaurant? Am I the only one who understands that divided we cannot stand? Let's just all wear long robes, make sure we pray to be seen, and demand the best seat. It must be okay now because everyone is doing it! Everyone called by God to be a part of the fivefold ministry encounters the same problem. Why doesn't everyone else understand the importance of their particular calling and ministry?

A church with a good pastor and good teachers, who have been grown spiritually, will always accept correction and are always ready to follow God's directions. There is a spirit of discernment discerning God's voice in the spiritually-mature churches. The poor in spiritual growth will not, and simply can't, understand this. Their pastors can't, either, and many are simply jealous. If this is the situation, there is never any growth beyond the pastor's present state of spirituality. Pastors will not grow, the church will not grow, and the congregation will not grow. This is a natural feeling, and is further enforced when the pastor's job and their position or reputation is also in question.

These types of feelings are not present in a pastor who has had time to be in the Word of God and has been grown under a mature, fully-grown, and capable pastor. These are pastors that were able to grow among other men and women of God at various conferences and outreaches. Churches, put your pastors into the Son and among those in Him!

There are many churches across this nation that have well-meaning pastors that were never matured under a grown pastor. These are the pastors that struggle with most of these issues. They are now in a position that require them to be the head, but they really never received what was required to be a pastor. I believe many of these pastors were really evangelists and good teachers that ended up pastoring a church. Because they need good examples to follow, we must give them every opportunity to be with other pastors who are grown, mature, and successful. Every pastor needs relationships that they can call on for assistance when needed. Many times this cannot be from anyone in their church, and the congregations need to appreciate this and provide for this. This is hard for many to accept: that their pastor often needs someone besides them.

I have found the most critical hindrance in growing a pastor is within the body of Christ—where you and I are not being and doing what we are supposed to! Yes, of course there are too many pastors doing a poor job. We must also acknowledge there are even more pastors that are devils in the pulpit. Both of these situations are unacceptable and will only stop when we quit supporting and listening to them. Every one of them are there because of the lack of our spiritual discernment. The nonproducing pastors, however, need an opportunity to be made whole. Remember the parable of our Lord:

> Then said he unto the dresser of his vineyard, Behold, these three years I come seeking fruit on this fig tree, and find none: cut it down; why cumbereth it the ground? And he answering said unto him, Lord, let it alone this year also, till I shall dig about it, and dung it: and if it bear fruit, well: and if not, then after that thou shalt cut it down.
>
> —Luke 13:7–9

When our pastors are not producing, we need to dig about them, fertilize them, and give them time in the Son. But also know it's not about them. It is about the fruit that is not harvested. Time is running out. People are dying to hell's damnation every second of every day! We cannot waste time! Just be sure we put a limit on the time to produce; Jesus did and so should the churches today. We are a part, but it is up to our pastors to be what God called them to be and to do. This is a business that is to produce souls. If they can't or won't become one, get one that will.

If your pastor is a devil, you'll only know by the Word of God. They will be so very close to the real thing that, to some, it will be hard to tell. Some might even be good pastors and have been possessed by the devil with little changes here and there until you're deceived and lost. Almost all the time, these devils will start acting like Jesus but will begin making inappropriate decisions, like who should or should not be in church. They will be trying to get rid of persons who know the Word of God.

When you see a pastor belittle and try to silence someone who is a maturing Christian and is knowledgeable in the Word of God, *watch out!* He will take the body of Christ in a direction that will look and appear godly, but it never really will be of God! Nor will it ever expand the kingdom of God! Every church and every pastor of God will be growing, expanding, producing, raising up, and sending. The church of the devil will keep everything inside itself, spending time, money, and energy on endless programs that make everyone feel good but never do much about winning souls. This is a trap! It is so deceiving as it appears to be so close to the real thing—but it is not! We must let the Word of God be our authority and guide to what the real thing is:

> Ye shall know them by their fruits. Do men gather grapes of thorns, or figs of thistles? Even so every good tree bringeth forth good fruit; but a corrupt tree bringeth forth evil fruit. A good tree cannot bring forth evil fruit, neither can a corrupt tree bring forth good fruit. Every tree that bringeth not forth good fruit is hewn down, and cast into the fire. Wherefore by their fruits ye shall know them.
>
> —MATTHEW 7:16–20

> And no marvel; for Satan himself is transformed into an angel of light. Therefore it is no great thing if his ministers also be transformed as the ministers of righteousness; whose end shall be according to their works.
>
> —2 CORINTHIANS 11:14–15

Please, brothers and sisters, we must at this very important time in history understand this. We have devils in our pulpits and we must expose them and get rid of them. Expose them by their works, or fruits, which will be the lack of either for God's kingdom. We must not let how we feel enter into the decision. Do we think they are not going to be loving? Do we think we would find them repulsive or be people we would not like? They will be some of the most loving, kind, likeable people we will ever meet. It will take mature Christians with their eyes and heart on God, to discern these demons, and they will deceive most. *God give us pastors of You to teach and help us!*

> For there shall arise false Christs, and false prophets, and shall shew great signs and wonders; insomuch that, if it were possible, they shall deceive the very elect. Behold, I have told you before.
>
> —MATTHEW 24:24–25

> And many false prophets shall rise, and shall deceive many.
>
> —MATTHEW 24:11

And Jesus answered and said unto them, Take heed that no man deceive you. For many shall come in my name, saying, I am Christ; and shall deceive many.

—MATTHEW 24:4–5

I have presented several topics of immense importance in this book, and I would like to conclude by restating, as accurately as possible, the things God put in my heart to write and share. Please understand that I am not an author. I am far from proficient in the use of language skills. I greatly lack in every needed area.

This book is the result of many selfless hours of correction by my wife. I say this to thank you for struggling though the messenger's shortcomings and pray you received the message in spite of me!

Many will have found these words harsh, much too pointed and unyielding. They are probably correct; however, I refuse to waste time. Please understand—I am passionate about your soul, and, as I have said, your feelings need to be someone else's concern, not mine. I must say here I was called into the ministry over thirty years ago, I did not go, and chose to be a servant to Satan instead of God. My life for Satan was fast and fierce, manifesting his works regularly. Like all sinners, I am forgiven by the grace of God. However, it is a fact that there are many in hell because of my decision. I therefore have committed to God that I will go faster for Him than I did for Satan. I, therefore, am in a big hurry and have no desire to be around those who do not want to keep up. I know I will never be able to catch up, or even make up for my deplorable life, but with God's help, I at least plan to keep up! There may be others like me; I hope we can work together at breakneck speed, supernaturally. Will you join me?

My thoughts to follow, hopefully, clarify what I believe God is trying to tell us today. They are to help us grow and become what we need to be for God. I hope to inspire some to step out and up to new levels of spiritual servanthood. I am here to proclaim that this is the time and the hour to be serious, to become real about our Lord and King. To bring awareness to our real conditions, as well as awareness of what God's Word really says about these conditions. These thoughts will be short and to the point, benefiting only those who are willing to change by realizing what we must become and do. This is to those who agree that the continuation of the nonproducing churches must stop. This is to those who understand that each of us is a part of the solution. I now am speaking to those that know they have been put in this place, at this time in history, by God.

Pastors will come in many different styles and personalities, and they will have different priorities. This is a good and desirable thing. Please, however, understand there are only two types of pastors: those called by God, and those that are placed by Satan who are his demons.

> And no marvel; for Satan himself is transformed into an angel of light. Therefore it is no great thing if his ministers also be transformed as the ministers of righteousness; whose end shall be according to their works.
>
> —2 Corinthians 11:14–15

We must realistically look at our world, our country, and our schools and know how prevalent this is. Understand that God has told us about this so we can be aware and, as always, we can overcome. We, the called servants of God, must stop thinking inside the box and start thinking with the mind of Christ.

Churches as a whole are not what God has ordained them to be. Many churches are more denominational than godly and are controlled by the spirit of religion. The large denominations can and will be a powerful force in these last days. We all need to help shed any creeds or codes put above God's Word. Godly churches, those that are truly called to become the bride of Christ, will not be divisive or exclusionary. The churches must unite and work together, and they must start now. Real churches will have God's vision and be working in God's will. They will know they are but a small part of a whole body, thankful just to be a part.

> For by one Spirit are we all baptized into one body, whether we be Jews or Gentiles, whether we be bond or free; and have been all made to drink into one Spirit. For the body is not one member, but many.
>
> —1 Corinthians 12:13–14

> That he might present it to himself a glorious church, not having spot, or wrinkle, or any such thing; but that it should be holy and without blemish.
>
> —Ephesians 5:27

This is the last-day church and we all need to be working toward being what God wants. The churches must become about the business of God, accomplishing what God set forth for our churches to produce, and the product is souls.

Christians is a term used by millions and millions, of which many, if not most, are heathens heading for hell faster than the spirit of stinginess shows up at the offering time in our services. That, by the way, is one of the fastest, most powerful demons that Satan has ever sent, it keeps untold thousands out of the place where God can use and bless them. Real Christians should be screaming "Identity theft," exposing frauds for what they are. Consider how many souls are lost by their false examples of Christianity.

> Verily, verily, I say unto you, If a man keep my saying, he shall never see death.
>
> —John 8:51

> A good man out of the good treasure of his heart bringeth forth that which is good; and an evil man out of the evil treasure of his heart bringeth forth that which is evil: for of the abundance of the heart his mouth speaketh. And why call ye me, Lord, Lord, and do not the things which I say? Whosoever cometh to me, and heareth my sayings, and doeth them, I will shew you to whom he is like: He is like a man which built an house, and digged deep, and laid the foundation on a rock: and when the flood arose, the stream beat vehemently upon that house, and could not shake it: for it was founded upon a rock. But he that heareth, and doeth not, is like a man that without a foundation built an house upon the earth; against which the stream did beat vehemently, and immediately it fell; and the ruin of that house was great.
>
> —Luke 6:45–49

We see false, deceiving, proclaimed Christians all the time and do nothing. I have stated how we need to conduct ourselves as a business, and have used McDonald's as an example in this book. Go to any corner of this country, or even the world, and sell hamburgers by putting up a sign that says "McDonald's" and see what happens and how fast. If a bunch of businesspeople are so concerned about protecting the image of a hamburger, why isn't the church protecting the name we know that is set above all names: Jesus the Christ?

I must end, especially since this book is about growing pastors, by pointing out their biggest problem. The pastors being raised today, along with those that are already in place, all have a major problem and we, the church, must expose it for what it is. It is a serious problem and everyone of them has the same problem. We cannot only discover this problem, but see it up close and reveal it for what it is. Go look in the mirror. There is the problem with the churches, the pastors, and with our families. Everyone of us is rotten to the core, self-centered, controlling, unchanging. We are simply worthless to ourselves, to God, and to our struggling pastors. We all get goose bumps thinking God so loved us that He gave His Son for us, but God also said:

> And it repented the LORD that he had made man on the earth, and it grieved him at his heart. And the LORD said, I will destroy man whom I have created from the face of the earth; both man, and beast, and the creeping thing, and the fowls of the air; for it repenteth me that I have made them.
>
> —GENESIS 6:6–7

From the spiritual condition of our world, we haven't changed much and we know from the Scriptures that God doesn't change. We have so little to offer our pastors, and they have such an enormous task. If most all of them were just assigned to fix me, they would have an awful hard task with such little reward; and then they also need to fix you. What kind of a job do you think that is?

For those of us who want to be a pastor-grower, we must grow up. God, please help everyone like me—they need help too!

To Contact the Author

Ronald L. Gordon
Victory in Business
7 West Main Street
Suite 1200
Apopka, FL 32703

E-mail: Ron@RLGordoncompany.com